BEHIND THE BAR

50 COCKTAIL RECIPES
FROM THE WORLD'S
MOST ICONIC HOTELS

ALIA AKKAM

BEHIND
THE
BAR

50 COCKTAIL RECIPES
FROM THE WORLD'S
MOST ICONIC HOTELS

Illustrations
by Evi-O.Studio

Hardie Grant

BOOKS

CONTENTS

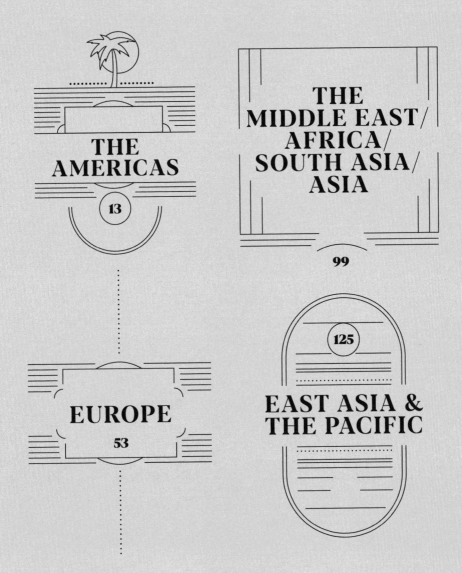

THE
AMERICAS

13

THE
MIDDLE EAST/
AFRICA/
SOUTH ASIA/
ASIA

99

EUROPE

53

125

EAST ASIA &
THE PACIFIC

INTRODUCTION

GET TO KNOW STAND-OUT HOTEL BARS FROM AROUND THE WORLD, AND THEIR RECIPES FOR LIBATIONS THAT YOU CAN WHIP UP AT YOUR HOME BAR WITH EASE.

KOLLÁZS, the restaurant inside the Four Seasons Hotel Gresham Palace Budapest, has its own entrance, but when I visit I prefer to reach it through the lobby. This way I can look up at the restored glass cupola overhead and the mosaic tiles at my feet, savouring a taste of what the building was like when it first opened at the beginning of the 20th century. I make my way past the waiters, scuttling across the floor with plates of the signature octopus, scallop and sausage atop a bed of paprika potatoes, to the circular bar dominating one side of the dining room. I sit down – as I often do – alone, yet surrounded by strangers.

There is banter with the bartenders, eventually leading to a beautiful cocktail set before me, and then, as my thoughts drift, I find calm in the anonymity. None of the people around me know who I am. Here, I can really be anyone – the person I want them to think I am, the person I might still become.

Certainly, I find comfort in a no-frills neighbourhood bar, too – watching the same locals order the same too-chilled glasses of white wine from the same surly barman – but I know I am not the only one who relishes the hotel bar for the enigmatic aura it conjures, for its power to instil in you the child-like belief in kismet you thought was long gone. Spending the night in a swank hotel room is a fleeting, glamorous experience and the hotel bar, heightened by the knowledge that there is an endless parade of guests slipping in and out of the sumptuous king-size beds above, is just as seductive a setting; the stream of possibilities just as infinite. That is why I wrote this book: to celebrate 50 of the world's finest hotel bars – some of which you might never have heard of – and their distinctive and colourful legacies.

In the 1920s, when some American bartenders fled to Europe in the wake of Prohibition, hotel bars were hotspots, places where celebrities and the well-heeled convened. Much of that magic still clings to certain properties and is cleverly reinterpreted at others. To understand the pull of the hotel bar, however, one must understand the evolution of the hotel.

Bill Kimpton opened the Clarion Bedford Hotel in San Francisco in 1981 (the first location of his soon-to-thrive Kimpton Hotel & Restaurant Group, known for its gratis 'Wine Hour' receptions, animal-print bathrobes, and friendly, informal service in every location) and the era of the boutique hotel was unofficially born. Three years later, Ian Schrager and his late business partner Steve Rubell, the genius New York club kings behind Studio 54 and later The Palladium, elevated the model on the East Coast and unveiled the see-and-be-seen-at Morgans New York. At this minimalist Andrée-Putman-designed hotel, the lobby was no longer a utilitarian check-in point, but a sizzling social hub. A similar velvet rope kind of flash (coincidentally the velvet rope, that ubiquitous form of crowd control, was brought to new heights at Studio 54 in the late 70s to ward off the riffraff) engulfed the avant-garde Royalton, Schrager and Rubell's next New York hotel (the first designed by the madcap Philippe Starck) in 1988. Three years later still, Gerber Group debuted The Whiskey bar at Schrager's Paramount Hotel and the perception of hotels as sources of electrifying nightlife was sealed.

Other milestones include the first of Chip Conley's Joie de Vivre hotels, which premiered in San Francisco (the brand is no longer Conley's; it's now part of the Hyatt portfolio); André Balazs readied Chateau Marmont for the scandalous Hollywood set; and Claus Sendlinger, keen to give small, good-looking hotels a voice, co-founded Design Hotels in 1993. W Hotels and Standard Hotels both arrived on the scene in 1998, giving young party people even more chances to romp around in style. A year later, the first Ace Hotel – a magnet for the on-a-budget creative class – was spawned from a one-time Seattle halfway house. All of these brands exhibited a different ethos, but their commitment to unconventionality was the common thread, proving that hotels could be memorable, not mundane. They placed a premium on design and, through their bars, they mesmerised the local community as much as the short-lived nomads. No longer did a hotel bar seem out-of-touch – the domain of the bejewelled affluent – nor did it remain the dingy domain of the business traveller who came around for perfunctory pours of bourbon.

The rise of the boutique hotel coincided with a universal shift in cocktails, from the morass of artificially flavoured mixers, soda guns and too-sweet drinks that were par for the course in the 1970s and 80s, to the made-from-scratch mindset that is fortunately abundant today.

As so much of the soulful past gives way to the slick and the bland, it's an important time to honour the bars that have survived the ages, the ones chock-full of character even if their drinks aren't the most ravishing, and the stirring 'modern classics' that may not have a long heritage bolstering their names, but flaunt quality in spades.

STAND OUT

Hotels
from the Americas, Europe, Africa, the Middle East, Asia and the Pacific

ACCOMPANIED BY

Cocktail recipes
directly from their bars

THE INS AND OUTS
OF THE BOOK

HOW TO USE THIS BOOK

On these pages, you will get to know stand-out hotels from the Americas, Europe, Africa, the Middle East, Asia and the Pacific accompanied by recipes directly from their bars. Some are straightforward, some are more time-consuming and complex, but with a little patience you should be able to track down most ingredients.

Although I mention how a bar specifically makes the drinks, I also note when they've been adapted in this book for the reader's ease. Likewise, many of the establishments call for the use of a particular brand in their creations. I have pointed these out to honour the bars' recipes – and the bartender's preference for a product – but if you can't track down a bottle that isn't widely available, don't fret; you can swap in, say, another whisky as you see fit.

· · · · · · · · · · ·

In the book you will constantly see **simple syrup** listed as an ingredient. It's a breeze to whip this up at home, and the same version can be applied to any cocktail that asks for it. A building block to numerous drinks, it's essentially sugar water, melding one part sugar with one part water (if this standard measurement varies, it's noted in the respective recipes). To achieve this convenient 1:1 ratio, simply combine a cup of water with a cup of granulated sugar in a saucepan. Bring them to a boil and stir together until dissolved over a medium heat, then measure out the amount noted in the recipe. After making a round of cocktails, store the remainder of the syrup in a glass jar for up to two weeks in the refrigerator until the next batch beckons.

· · · · · · · · · · ·

Armed with a basic bar tool kit – shaker, strainer, jigger, bar spoon, muddler, ice tongs – you should be well on your way to hosting a boozy dinner party.

· · · · · · · · · · ·

Finally, interspersed throughout the book are feature spreads that will give you a deeper understanding of hotel bar culture.

THE
AMERICAS

13

THE AMERICAS

In 1954, bartender Ramón 'Monchito' Marrero was credited with creating the holiday-in-a-glass Piña Colada at the Caribe Hilton in San Juan, Puerto Rico. The rum libation, with coconut cream, double (heavy) cream, pineapple juice and crushed ice was transporting, and exactly the kind of thrill bar-goers of the past looked forward to having brighten their long-planned vacations. Marrero's Piña Colada isn't the only cocktail rumoured to have been invented at a hotel bar, but its simplicity underscores the basic desires of guests and how hotels are well poised to fulfil them.

The cocktail craze that took hold in the States during the 2000s, and naturally spread north to Canada and south to Latin America, has yet to loosen its grip, and the bar stock in this region, including those in hotels, is much better for it. Bartenders use stellar ingredients now, and just like that 1950s Piña Colada did, a perfectly sculpted sphere of ice and piquant homemade syrups are what bring smiles these days. Hotel bars in the Americas may possess a certain razzle-dazzle, but the good ones know it's only one part of the game.

No. 1

Pisco Sour

BAR INGLÉS AT
COUNTRY CLUB
LIMA HOTEL,
LIMA, PERU

INGREDIENTS

120 ml (4 fl oz) pure Quebranta pisco
30 ml (1 fl oz) freshly squeezed
  lemon juice
30 ml (1 fl oz) simple syrup (page 11)
dash of egg white
Angostura bitters, to garnish

METHOD

Combine all the ingredients in
a cocktail shaker filled with ice
and shake vigorously. Strain into
a chilled goblet and add 1–2 drops
of Angostura bitters to garnish.

When it opened in 1927, Country Club Lima
Hotel resembled a sweeping Spanish colonial
mansion — a style that was then very much
in vogue among Lima's high-society circles,
despite Peru's liberation from Spain in the
1820s. Located in the fashionable San Isidro
neighbourhood, it was once complete with
a circa-1940s polo field and, in its heyday, it
lured in luminaries such as Nelson Rockefeller,
Ava Gardner and John Wayne, who first met his
third wife here. If they hobnobbed, they likely
all did so with a Pisco Sour by their side in the
wood-panelled Bar Inglés, which calls to mind
an English gentlemen's club.

Years later, Peru's frothy flagship cocktail
remains the go-to drink order, but curious
tipplers may want those still-dapper bartenders
to pour them another pisco specialty for
their second round, such as the refreshing
'Chilcano' with ginger ale, or the 'Chicha Sour'
brightened by Peruvian purple corn.

A Peruvian history lesson isn't taught
solely at the bar but throughout the property.
Three hundred pieces of colonial art donated
by the Pedro de Osma Museum delineate the
country's vast artistic legacy, along with the
murals illuminating Andean textiles that hang
over the guest-room beds.

THE AMERICAS

BEHIND THE BAR

No. 2

Carioca Iced Tea

POOL BAR AT BELMOND
COPACABANA PALACE,
RIO DE JANEIRO, BRAZIL

INGREDIENTS

20 ml (⅔ fl oz) cachaça
20 ml (⅔ fl oz) vodka
20 ml (⅔ fl oz) gin
20 ml (⅔ fl oz) freshly squeezed
 lemon juice
20 ml (⅔ fl oz) simple syrup
 (page 11)
50 ml (1¾ fl oz) freshly brewed
 tea (the bar uses mate, but any
 chilled, citrus-forward black
 tea would work)
mint leaves and lemon twist,
 to garnish

METHOD

Combine all the ingredients in a
cocktail shaker filled with ice and
shake vigorously for 10 seconds.
Strain into a collins or highball
glass filled with ice, then garnish
with mint leaves and a lemon twist.

Illustrious dancing duo Fred Astaire and
Ginger Rogers were first paired together
on screen in *Flying Down to Rio*, a 1933
musical-comedy-romance that introduced
audiences to both the forehead-touching
dance craze 'Carioca', and the notion of Rio
de Janeiro as a cinematic South-American
getaway. At the centre of this fantasy
is the Copacabana Palace.

Now Belmond Copacabana Palace,
the hotel opened in 1923, directly across
from its beautiful (soon to be world-famous)
namesake beach. Designed in the Beaux-
Arts style by French architect Joseph Gire,
it attracted jet-setters eager to soak up
luxe tropical vibes – Orson Welles, Brigitte
Bardot and Mick Jagger all holed up here over
the years. And a conversation at the hotel
between Barry Manilow and lyricist Bruce
Sussman supposedly sparked their 1978 hit
song 'Copacabana'. The domed Golden Room,
where Ella Fitzgerald and Nat King Cole once
performed, is now a private events venue,
but the spectacular swimming pool is still
cloaked in Old World glamour. At the Pool
Bar, libations feature Brazilian ingredients
such as white cachaça mixed with guarana,
a cumaru-fruit-infused-gin Negroni, and a
cashew-pulp Bellini.

No. 3

Hotel Nacional Riff

HOTEL NACIONAL
DE CUBA, HAVANA

Created by Erik Adkins

INGREDIENTS

45 ml (1½ fl oz) Banks 7 Golden
  Age rum (Barbancourt 8-year-
  old rum also works well)
25 ml (¾ fl oz) freshly squeezed
  lime juice
25 ml (¾ fl oz) Small Hand Foods
  pineapple gum syrup
15 ml (½ fl oz) Rothman & Winter
  apricot liqueur
small dash of Angostura bitters
lime twist, to garnish

METHOD

Combine all the ingredients in
a cocktail shaker filled with ice
and shake vigorously. Strain into
a chilled coupe glass and garnish
with a lime twist.

During the 1920s, in the grim days of
Prohibition, US bartenders eager to escape
the oppressive booze ban opened their own
boîtes in Havana. It was amid this vortex of
creativity (a time when American Eddie Woelke
was credited with inventing the El Presidente
cocktail at the Jockey Club – he possibly came
up with the rum-based Mary Pickford, too) that
Hotel Nacional de Cuba, aimed at tourists from
the States, opened in 1930.

Designed by McKim, Mead & White,
the New York architects behind projects
including the Brooklyn Museum and Columbia
University, the Nacional was a stately
building with views onto Havana's harbour
and Morro Castle. There were tennis courts,
a salt-water swimming pool, and a bar that
amplified Havana's reputation as the 'Paris
of the Caribbean', with guests like Rita
Hayworth, Frank Sinatra and Marlon Brando.
Old-fashioned Cuban elements, such as the
tiles, brass and mahogany in the lobby, the
lush gardens and, of course, the memorabilia-
packed bar, all summon a pre-Castro Havana.

The cocktail of choice – rumoured to have
been created for the hotel by its American
bartender, Wil P. Taylor – blended white rum
with pineapple juice and apricot liqueur, and
there have been numerous versions since,
including the recipe with gold rum that Charles
H. Baker Jr. included in his seminal travelogue-
cum-cookbook, *The Gentleman's Companion.*

The original recipe – the Hotel Nacional –
calls for pineapple juice, but in this riff (known
as Hotel Nacional Special C) by Erik Adkins,
bar director of The Slanted Door Group in San
Francisco, he opts for pineapple gum syrup,
imbuing the cocktail with a velvety feel.

HOTEL NACIONAL DE CUBA,
HAVANA, CUBA

MEET ME IN THE LOBBY

Twenty years ago, a guest might have checked into a 'luxury hotel' expecting copious swathes of veined marble in their bathroom, a room-service club sandwich formally presented underneath a silver cloche and a plush terry-cloth robe draped over the king-size bed. This uniform approach to top-tier hospitality worked in the past, but with the terms 'boutique' and 'lifestyle hotel' constantly bandied about today, the lines are now blurred. Luxury is subtlety; it's more personalised than ever. That means guests are less concerned with one-size-fits-all grandeur and wrapping themselves in high thread-count sheets than they are with the hotel's distinct point of view. How is this property impacting the community? How is it different from its neighbour with the equally thronged lobby of laptop-toting day drinkers up the street?

Often, this translates to pared-down (and gentler on the wallet), thoughtfully designed rooms that are bolstered by a strongly defined cultural and culinary ethos that unfurls in its public spaces. The modern-day hotel bar, then, helps contribute to an overall robust mixology scene while redefining luxury for guests who value fun over pretence.

Consider Portland, Oregon. Inside Hotel deLuxe is the Driftwood Room, a holdover from its days as the Regency-style Hotel Mallory. In the 1950s, locals came to the crystal-chandelier-appointed hotel for billiards and cigars. Now, even though it looks lifted from a retro Paramount set with its voluptuous banquettes and ribbed ceiling, the Driftwood Room is ultimately a relaxed joint, where dressed-down couples sneak away for cheeky absinthe-fountain service and happy-hour Champagne cocktails such as the 'Elizabeth Taylor' with crème de violette.

Just a few minutes away is Ace Hotel Portland, home to the laidback restaurant and bar Clyde Common. This is where bar manager Jeffrey Morgenthaler (you can also find him around the corner at the subterranean Pépé le Moko), author of *Drinking Distilled: A User's Manual* and *The Bar Book: Elements of Cocktail Technique*, first created the still-going-strong 'Barrel-Aged Negroni' at the end of 2009. Other cocktails, such as the 'Southbound Suarez' (reposado tequila, lime, agave, Becherovka, house-made horchata), keep the mix of visitors and Portlanders seated at the communal tables happy. As Morgenthaler sums it up: 'We wanted a space that was simple and unadorned, where the food and the drink and the service would shine. We just try to make sure everyone is comfortable and having a great time.'

Everyone is similarly at ease at The Drake Hotel in Toronto's West Queen West neighbourhood. The property is an incubator of local, national and international art, with a proper performance venue in place, and that creativity extends to the lounge and mural-covered rooftop Sky Yard, where an artistic crew convene over drinks such as the '92nd Street' (Monkey Shoulder Scotch, green Chartreuse, apple sencha tea, green curry leaf and vanilla seltzer).

One of the most masterful examples of unexpected liquor luxury is Broken Shaker, the bar first conceived as a pop-up by Bar Lab's

Gabe Orta and Elad Zvi. The first permanent post arrived in 2012 at Freehand Miami, a low-key hotel with souped-up social hostel vibes and bunk rooms available for packs of friends. Immediately, the beguiling courtyard, which has the air of an off-kilter *Alice in Wonderland* garden party, filled up with locals and tourists. There are now Broken Shaker bars at Freehand hotels in Chicago, Los Angeles and New York, and whether it's for an 'Apples to Oranges' (Don Julio reposado tequila, Campari, spiced orange cordial, sparkling cider) sipped on a New-York rooftop or a poolside 'Neon Nights' (Vida mezcal, Ancho Verde, Aperol, burnt citrus and togarashi cordial, wood-sorrel tincture, fresh lime juice) at the old Commercial Exchange building in downtown LA, Broken Shaker is always packed.

'We love the balance between high-brow and low-. The person who pays $20 a night for a bed at Freehand can exist in the bar alongside the person that lives across the street in a luxurious home and is a regular guest,' says managing partner Orta. Managing partner Zvi adds, 'We have something for everyone. The daily house punch goes for $8; for those looking to spend more, there are even $350 speciality bottles of Champagne. Both guests are welcome and we treat them the same.'

Madame Rambouillet's 17th-century French salons inspired The Ramble Hotel, in Denver's River North Art District. After guests leave their rooms with the antique Persian rugs and wideplank hickory floors, the mission is, just like Rambouillet's intimate gatherings,

to gab, learn and share within the confines of the hotel. Death & Co, the second location to follow the New York flagship by Alex Day, Dave Kaplan and Ravi DeRossi, plays a pivotal role in this exchange, with drinks such as the 'Wabi-Sabi' (High West Silver Western Oat whiskey, Japanese gin, white chocolate, wasabi, coconut, lemon, matcha) savoured from velvet couches.

'We've always thought of Death & Co as more than the four walls of the original East Village location. To us, Death & Co is more about a perspective on cocktails and hospitality – a way of working, how we should treat our guests and our team, an aesthetic for creative but elegantly reserved offerings – and we've been excited to express that in other forms for years, especially within the distinctly unique energy of a hotel,' explains Day. 'In Denver, we're given a chance to explore Death & Co's voice in so many ways: your first sip of coffee in the morning, a casual afternoon low ABV cocktail, an outdoor bar in the summer, or a deeply immersive evening cocktail experience with delicious food – so many creative opportunities, but always understandable as Death & Co. In that way, I think our success at Death & Co Denver and its integration into The Ramble Hotel is tied to our strong collective vision as a team and an almost child-like excitement for the many ways we can express it.'

Luxury is subtlety; it's more personalised than ever.

No. 4

Jamaican Manhattan

POOL BAR & GRILL AT
ROCKHOUSE HOTEL & SPA,
NEGRIL, JAMAICA

INGREDIENTS

60 ml (2 fl oz) Wray & Nephew
  Jamaican brandy
30 ml (1 fl oz) sweet vermouth
4 dashes of Angostura bitters
1 cherry, to garnish

METHOD

Combine all the ingredients in
a mixing glass filled with ice and
stir. Strain into a chilled Martini
glass and garnish with a cherry.

Rockhouse embodies an island paradise, what with its plethora of stone, thatch and wood that echo the jungle landscape – furnishings for its rooms, suites and villas are made in an on-site woodworking shop. Perched on Negril's dramatic coral cliffs, this eco-friendly boutique hotel opened in 1973, when it was a hangout for Bob Marley and Bob Dylan. In 1994, when the current Australian owner took over the property, he ensured that it wouldn't lose any of that soul. Instead, the hotel deepened its connection to Jamaica by starting a foundation that helps local children through renovating schools and libraries.

Four-poster beds beg a lie-in, but do rise, if only for a dip in the infinity pool and meals in the three restaurants and bars, which integrate greens from the organic garden into dishes and drinks. In anticipation of sunset, hightail it to the Pool Bar & Grill and gaze upon the Caribbean in the company of a 'Jamaican Manhattan' or cooling 'Jahjito', which is made with the island's own Appleton white rum and combines with mint leaves, lime, sugar and soda water.

ROCKHOUSE HOTEL & SPA, NEGRIL, JAMAICA

THE AMERICAS

No. 5

Billy the Kid

FIFTY MILS AT
FOUR SEASONS HOTEL
MEXICO CITY, MEXICO

INGREDIENTS

30 ml (1 fl oz) Bulleit Bourbon
  with Butter Fat Wash*
30 ml (1 fl oz) Zubrowka vodka
45 ml (1½ fl oz) Caramel Tea**
20 ml (⅔ fl oz) lime juice
25 ml (¾ fl oz) Saffron and
  Cinnamon Syrup†
2 dashes of Angostura bitters

* For the Bulleit Bourbon with Butter
  Fat Wash (makes 1 litre/34 fl oz):
1 kg (2 lb 4 oz) melted butter
750 ml (25 fl oz) Bulleit bourbon

** For the Caramel Tea
  (makes 1 litre/34 fl oz):
75 g (2½ oz) rooibos, vanilla
  or caramel tea
1 litre (34 fl oz) freshly boiled water

† For the Saffron and Cinnamon Syrup
  (makes 1 litre/34 fl oz):
100 g (3½ oz) cinnamon sticks
100 g (3½ oz) sugar
pinch of saffron
1 litre (34 fl oz) water

METHOD

For the Bulleit Bourbon, combine the ingredients, then pour into a container and freeze overnight. The following day, skim off the hardened layer of butter. Strain the bourbon into a sterilised bottle.

For the Caramel Tea, combine the ingredients and steep for 5 minutes, then strain and chill until needed.

For the Saffron and Cinnamon Syrup, combine the ingredients in a saucepan and heat for 5 minutes until the sugar has dissolved. Strain into a sterilised bottle and chill until needed.

Combine all the ingredients in a shaker filled with ice and shake vigorously. Double strain into a mug filled with large ice cubes.

Mexico City teems with vibrant bars – secretive, polished mixology dens, no-frills cantinas devoted to knocking back ice-cold cervezas and bartender favourites such as Licorería Limantour, making it one of Latin America's most seductive nightlife capitals.

Fifty Mils, inside the hacienda-style Four Seasons Hotel close to 'Bosque de Chapultepec', where guests are welcomed into a courtyard thronging with fruit trees, arrived on the scene in 2015, and was quickly recognised as one of the best places in the city to savour a cocktail. Drinks here are complex: the 'Bugs Bunny', for instance, melds Tanqueray 10 gin with carrot juice, lemongrass syrup, fresh cactus and Fernet perfume; in the 'Ofrenda', Zacapa 23 rum is paired with tamarind pulp, grilled pineapple juice and avocado-leaf bitters. Opt for a classic Manhattan and even that will come to the table with a distinctive flourish: it's served inside a hollow ice cube that the bartender confidently cracks open before guests' eyes.

INGREDIENTS

45 ml (1½ fl oz) Yola mezcal
25 ml (¾ fl oz) freshly squeezed
lime juice
25 ml (¾ fl oz) mango purée
(ideally Boiron or Perfect Purée)
15 ml (½ fl oz) Giffard Abricot du
Roussillon apricot liqueur
7.5 ml (¼ fl oz) Campari
7.5 ml (¼ fl oz) cane syrup (2 parts
organic cane sugar to 1 part water)
Chilli Salt*, to garnish
1 lime wheel and wedge, to garnish

*For the Chilli Salt:
1 teaspoon Tajin chilli and lime
seasoning
½ teaspoon cayenne pepper
½ teaspoon sugar

METHOD

Combine all the ingredients in
a cocktail shaker filled with ice
and shake vigorously. Fill a saucer
with the chilli salt mixture and rub
the lime edge around half of the
rim of a rocks glass. Dip the rim
of the glass into the chilli salt.
Fill the glass with ice, then strain
the cocktail into the glass. Garnish
with the lime wheel.

Unless you're planted in a red booth at
Musso & Frank Grill, retro Hollywood glitz
can feel elusive in today's sprawling LA. But,
walk out of that restaurant dating from 1919
and some ten minutes across Hollywood
Boulevard, past the 1920s movie palace
formerly known as Grauman's Chinese Theatre,
and there is The Hollywood Roosevelt, a hotel
where you can easily imagine a dewy Marilyn
Monroe reclining on a lounge chair.

In 1929, when the property was just two
years old, the first-ever Academy Awards
was held here in the form of a small, private
dinner. The celebrities, including Clark Gable
and Carole Lombard, who once resided in what
is now the rooftop penthouse, never stopped
coming. That dizzying spirit, reflected through
a contemporary lens, is what permeates The
Spare Room, where pals share bowls of Nanu
Nanu punch (Pierre Ferrand Cognac, apricot,
rooibos tea, spiced pineapple, lemon and
Domaine Chandon sparkling wine) before
hitting the vintage two-lane bowling alley.

Spend the day against a backdrop of palm
trees at the Tropicana Pool, graced with an
underwater mural painted by David Hockney,
then end it playing dominoes, snug on one of
The Spare Room's sofas with a potato vodka
and carrot-dill brine 'Salt and Vinegar Martini'.
It's the kind of carefree, off-set living that
bygone stars would surely approve of.

No. 6

Show Off

THE SPARE ROOM
AT THE HOLLYWOOD ROOSEVELT,
LOS ANGELES, USA

Created by Yael Vengroff

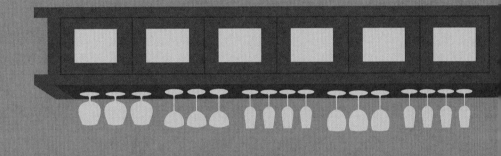

THE AMERICAS

BEHIND THE BAR

No. 7

Esperanto

THE HAWTHORNE
AT HOTEL
COMMONWEALTH,
BOSTON, USA

Created by Jackson Cannon

INGREDIENTS

60 ml (2 fl oz) Del Maguey
  Crema de Mezcal
25 ml (¾ fl oz) La Cigarrera
  Manzanilla sherry
15 ml (½ fl oz) Carpano Antica
  vermouth
1 dash of Regans' orange bitters
1 pared strip of lemon zest

METHOD

Add all the ingredients except
the lemon zest to a mixing glass
filled with ice and stir. Strain into
a chilled double old fashioned
glass, twist the lemon zest over
the drink to express the oils,
then discard.

Lucky are the folks who, after seeing a
Red Sox game at Fenway Park, need only
walk a few minutes over to Kenmore Square
to spend the night at Hotel Commonwealth.
If they're die-hard fans, they'll likely make
their way up to the 65-square-metre (700-
square-foot) suite chock-full of baseball
mementos. Yet there are so many others who
flock here, with nary a thought of sport nor
sleep, just to drink in The Hawthorne bar.

In what feels like an arty friend's living
room, with plenty of cushy seating that
seamlessly mingles zebra print with bright
orange, they reach for a 'Bookmark' listing
the evening's cocktails – maybe a demure
mid-century Champagne 'Air Mail', or maybe
a 'Grand Tour' with El Tesoro reposado tequila,
Amontillado sherry, pineapple and lime.

The Hawthorne opened in 2011, courtesy
of tireless bartender Jackson Cannon – a
well-travelled, music-loving booze scholar,
who first cemented the city's reputation for
exalted cocktails at Eastern Standard back
in 2005. Also inside Hotel Commonwealth,
this boisterous brasserie is where you'll find
oyster-gorging regulars asking for banana
daiquiris and rum old fashioneds. Consider
the understated Hawthorne, then, an evolution
of Cannon's mission to enlighten.

SPOTLIGHT:
DAVID ROCKWELL
*the connection between hospitality design
and performing arts*

ONE
EPHEMERAL
EVENING

Rockwell Group's portfolio of projects is vast, including restaurants, hotels, retail and products. The New York-based architecture and design practice, launched in 1984 by David Rockwell, is also renowned for its theatre work, imagining sets for Broadway hits such as She Loves Me *and* Kinky Boots. *For Rockwell – as he explains here – the connection between the realms of hospitality and performing arts is a fierce one. Hotel bars, for example, and the sweeping stage, are both propelled by a sense of transience, allowing the designer to create magic over and over again.*

Design is our filter to examine the world, and it informs everything that we do. Often, the lines between mediums and spaces aren't as rigid as we might think. Theatre and hospitality, for example, are intertwined in many ways, and this symbiotic relationship really drives our work. Just as with a performance, we approach everything we design from a place of narrative. We are telling a story and crafting a point of view; a unique world that's specific to the project. In both cases, you are exploring temporal structures, lighting, emotional connection and heightening the atmosphere for impact. We always ask ourselves at the beginning of a project, 'What is the story we are telling?' and the answer to that question informs every choice we make thereafter.

At Moxy Chelsea hotel in New York, for example, the story of the flower district weaves a powerful impression on the three amenities we designed. It's a modern fusion of botanically-inspired elements and Italian Futurism. The Fleur Room, an intimate rooftop bar on the 35th floor of the hotel, is one of my favourite spaces. An extruding bronze bar, recalling the chic precision of intimate bars found in Rome or Milan, contrasts floral accents such as inverted resin cones glowing with imbedded bouquets. These design choices may never be consciously recognised by many who encounter the space, but that doesn't mean they won't play on memory, spark specific feelings, and create a lasting impact on the guest experience.

Hotel bars are often the nexus of a space – the stage. They are where the action takes place and, often in the span of just 24 hours, can take on multiple roles and create a range of experiences. When we create communal spaces such as these, we apply many of the same concepts as set design.

For example, a sense of choreography – another element of theatre – can guide a guest's journey. A path through a hotel's public spaces with thresholds – transitional moments – are where the magic happens. For the Fairmont Royal York hotel in Toronto and Electric Lemon restaurant at the flagship Equinox Hotel in New York, we sought out those key transitional moments in the lobby, enabling them to transcend to bar and lounge areas. This creates a feeling of movement and flow; the bar space becoming its own world, able to expand or contract depending on volume or occasion.

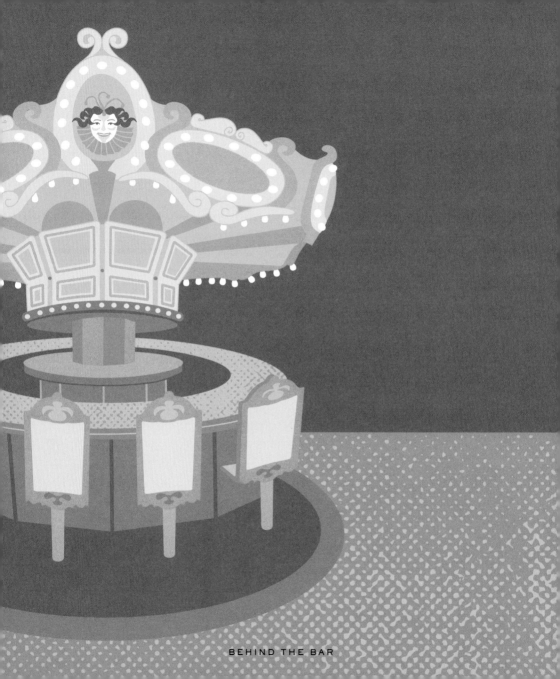

BEHIND THE BAR

No. 8

Vieux Carré

CAROUSEL BAR & LOUNGE
AT HOTEL MONTELEONE,
NEW ORLEANS, USA

INGREDIENTS

7.5 ml (¼ fl oz) Bénédictine
7.5 ml (¼ fl oz) Cognac
15 ml (½ fl oz) Sazerac rye whiskey
7.5 ml (¼ fl oz) sweet vermouth
3 drops of Angostura bitters
3 drops of Peychaud's bitters
lemon twist, to garnish

METHOD

Stir all the ingredients except the
lemon twist in a mixing glass filled
with ice. Strain into a chilled old
fashioned glass and garnish with
the twist of lemon.

After presiding over a Sicilian shoe factory,
Antonio Monteleone, like many enterprising
immigrants of his time, headed for America
with unbridled opportunity on his mind.
Settling in New Orleans, that ambition led to
opening Hotel Monteleone, overlooking the
French Quarter's Royal Street, in 1886. This
pool-topped grande dame is purportedly
abundant in haunted lairs, but beyond
that paranormal fascination there is the
equally intriguing Carousel Bar & Lounge,
where an ornate merry-go-round, seemingly
plucked from a carnival of yesteryear, is
the centrepiece. Set inside the whimsical
contraption is a circular bar accompanied by
25 colourful chairs covered in illustrations of
circus animals. Delightfully and imperceptibly,
every 15 minutes it revolves around the room.

Transcending mere feel-good gimmickry,
Carousel, spinning since 1949, has a luminous
literary past. Southern American scribes such
as Truman Capote (his mother went into labour
with him at the hotel), Tennessee Williams,
William Faulkner and Eudora Welty paid
inspiration-inducing visits here. Entertainers
including Liberace and Louis Prima, after their
performances in the hotel's now-shuttered
nightclub The Swan Room, also slipped into
the Carousel.

The boozy Vieux Carré, invented by the
hotel's head bartender Walter Bergeron in
1938, as well as that must-have-when-in-
the-Big-Easy Sazerac remain sought-after
concoctions from the charismatic, long-time
barman Marvin Allen.

With ingredients that nod to France, Italy,
the Caribbean and the United States, the Vieux
Carré (which literally translates to 'Old Square',
an homage to the French Quarter) reflects a
lively, multicultural New Orleans.

No. 9

Mint Julep

ROUND ROBIN BAR AT
INTERCONTINENTAL THE WILLARD
WASHINGTON, DC, USA

Adapted by Jim Hewes

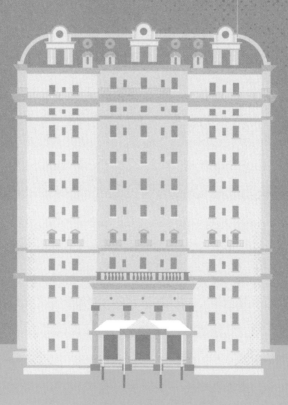

INGREDIENTS

60 ml (2 fl oz) bourbon
4–6 fresh mint leaves, plus
   a mint spring to garnish
1 teaspoon sugar
130 g (4½ oz/1 cup) crushed ice
30 ml (1 fl oz) San Pellegrino
   sparkling water
pinch of granulated or raw cane
   sugar, to garnish

METHOD

Using a spoon, muddler or the bottom of a butter knife, gently muddle the mint leaves and sugar with half of the bourbon in a Pilsner glass or brandy snifter for a minute or so until a 'tea' forms. Add half of the crushed ice and stir again, then top up the glass with the remaining crushed ice, keeping it tightly packed. Pour in the remaining bourbon and sparkling water, then garnish with a mint sprig and a sprinkling of sugar.

A Pennsylvania-Avenue landmark minutes away from the White House, the Willard has long been one of the capital's choice gathering spots for the crème de la crème of politics. Since 1847, Round Robin Bar (in what was then called Willard's City Hotel) has turned out cocktails for the likes of Mark Twain and Walt Whitman – the latter even called out the Willard's 'sumptuous bar' in a rousing speech to Union troops – as well as to countless gossip-fuelled employees of lobbying firms and US presidential administrations past.

Jim Hewes began tending the polished mahogany circular bar in 1986, when the hotel reopened deep in the conservative Ronald Reagan years. He's every bit the knowledgeable historian as he is the skillful bartender responsible for tweaking the beloved Mint Julep. The tufted leather, oak panelling and earthy green walls lined with portraits of such personalities of yore as Woodrow Wilson, expedited by a 'Papa Doble' (Hemingway Daiquiri) or Prohibition-era 'Bee's Knees' in hand, all conjure a riveting sensation of covert meetings and political discourse.

NINETEENTH-CENTURY KENTUCKY STATESMAN HENRY CLAY WAS BESOTTED WITH THE MINT JULEP, FIRST INTRODUCING IT TO WASHINGTONIANS AT ROUND ROBIN. COME SUMMER, THE BAR CONTINUES TO PUMP OUT THE ICY WARM-WEATHER QUENCHER NOW SYNONYMOUS WITH DERBY DAY SOIRÉES. ALTHOUGH MOST VERSIONS OF THE COCKTAIL ARE SERVED IN A PEWTER CUP, ROUND ROBIN PREFERS A PILSNER GLASS OR BRANDY SNIFTER TO FULLY ILLUMINATE THE BEAUTY OF THE DRINK.

No. 10

Bloody Mary

KING COLE BAR
AT ST REGIS
NEW YORK, USA

INGREDIENTS

30 ml (1 fl oz) vodka
60 ml (2 fl oz) tomato juice
1 dash of freshly squeezed
   lemon juice
2 pinches of celery salt
2 pinches of black pepper
2 pinches of cayenne pepper
3 dashes of Worcestershire sauce
lemon wedge, to garnish

METHOD

Combine the ingredients in a
cocktail shaker filled with ice
and shake vigorously. Strain into a
highball glass filled with ice cubes
and garnish with a lemon wedge.

Wealthy John Jacob Astor IV, the tycoon who perished in the Titanic disaster, opened The St Regis New York in 1904. The Beaux-Arts showcase of marble and Waterford crystal chandeliers was situated in a then-residential area of the city, much to the dismay of Vanderbilt Row denizens. If you're seated at King Cole Bar, which opened at the St Regis in 1932, it is likely that the expertly made drink placed before you will be a Bloody Mary, a cocktail that is often undeservedly reserved for brunch-time feasting.

King Cole Bar is considered the post-Prohibition birthplace of the Bloody Mary, or rather the 'Red Snapper'. When the drink debuted here, it was given this more dignified name to appease to the hotel's highfalutin guests. It's stuck ever since.

As a rite of passage, the signature drink can be ordered any time of the evening, simply dressed with lemon and shorn of celery stalks, pickle spears and olives – those clunky, intrusive garnishes that all too commonly mar a Bloody Mary these days.

Drink lore aside, the room stuns with a Maxfield Parrish mural hanging above the bar, its saturated hues bringing to life Old King Cole, that 'merry old soul' eternalised in nursery rhymes. Originally commissioned for Astor's Knickerbocker Hotel, the painting's throne-ensconced king, underscoring Astor's bravado, bears the hotelier's likeness.

FERNAND PETIOT, SUPPOSED INVENTOR OF THE TOMATO JUICE AND VODKA COCKTAIL, FIRST STARTED SERVING IT TO HIS GENTEEL GUESTS AT KING COLE BAR IN 1934. IT WAS CHRISTENED THE 'RED SNAPPER' – A FAR MORE ELEGANT ALTERNATIVE TO THE GAUCHE 'BLOODY MARY'.

THE AMERICAS

No. 11

Loisaida Avenue

THE NOMAD AND
ELEPHANT BARS
AT THE NOMAD HOTEL,
NEW YORK, USA

Created by Leo Robitschek

INGREDIENTS

15 ml (½ fl oz) simple syrup
(page 11)
15 ml (½ fl oz) green Chartreuse
25 ml (¾ fl oz) freshly squeezed
lemon juice
25 ml (¾ fl oz) Sombra mezcal
25 ml (¾ fl oz) Jalapeño-Infused
Tequila*
1 dash of Angostura bitters,
to garnish

*For the Jalapeño-Infused Tequila
(makes 750 ml/25 fl oz):
3 medium-sized jalapeños, diced
1 x 750 ml (25 fl oz) bottle Excellia
Blanco tequila

METHOD

For the Jalapeño-Infused Tequila,
steep the jalapeños and tequila
in a container for 5 minutes.
Taste the mixture to ensure that
the spice level is to your taste;
if you prefer a spicier end product,
allow to steep for longer. Strain
into a sterilised airtight container
and store in the refrigerator
indefinitely.

To make the cocktail, combine
all the ingredients except the
bitters in a cocktail shaker filled
with ice and shake vigorously.
Strain into a Nick & Nora glass,
then top the cocktail with a dash
of Angostura bitters.

Hospitality hit-makers, Sydell Group (The Line,
The Ned, Saguaro), first wowed New Yorkers
with the NoMad – a revamped, turn-of-the-
century Beaux-Arts building in Manhattan's
Madison Square North neighbourhood – in
2012. Even if visitors don't get a peek into
the Jacques Garcia-designed guest rooms,
reminiscent of a Parisian pied-à-terre with
free-standing clawfoot bathtubs and velvet-
and-damask-patterned screens, there is the
dimly-lit library to gawk at – a spiral staircase
imported from the South of France connecting
its two floors of wall-to-wall tomes. There is
also the eponymous restaurant, home to a
storied chicken-for-two stuffed with black
truffle and brioche foie gras.

The NoMad Bar, which has the air of a
gussied-up tavern and serves dry-aged beef
burgers to match, and The Elephant Bar – a
swirl of mahogany and leather that invites
multiple nightcaps – are just as romantic,
swelling with both hotel guests and locals
seeking out some of the city's most finely
wrought cocktails. With a flair for the savoury,
these creations deftly incorporate ingredients
such as olive oil-infused tequila, sheep's milk
yoghurt and horseradish. Despite the growth
of the NoMad brand, since expanding into Los
Angeles, Las Vegas and London, the New York
original thankfully feels at once timeless and
energised.

HOTEL BAR MAGIC

'Historically, the hotel was simply a place in which to rest; a place just for hotel guests. Now, however, the hotel has become a social hub; a place where everyone can gather. This is largely thanks to the hotel bar, which universally appeals. The legendary bars of the roaring twenties provided a blueprint for hotel bars: approachable and comfortable, yet incredibly glamorous and with a hint of intrigue. I've always sought to make the hotel bar feel special and a destination in its own right. By incorporating aspects such as a separate entrance and a concept that feels different from the rest of the hotel, the hotel bar is unique and appealing; it's a place of excitement.'

Martin Brudnizki, London- and New York-based founder of Martin Brudnizksi Design Studio, which has handled such bars as The Coral Room at The Bloomsbury Hotel in London; The Bar Room at The Beekman, A Thompson Hotel, in New York; and Doyle at the Dupont Circle hotel in Washington, DC.

• • • • • • • • • • •

'Part of the allure of hotel bars is that anything is possible. There is an extra level of intrigue with the mix of people who have been here before, are enjoying the freedom of travel, or shaking off a workday far away from their community. There is more of an openness to talk to a neighbour, or be adventurous with a drink order. I sometimes get the sense that people are trying out a different version of themselves. At Dear Irving on Hudson it is a big part of our philosophy to remember the first trip we saved up for, knowing that we are going to see many people visiting NYC for the first time who cannot truly be themselves at home, but here there is a possibility of feeling fulfilled, even for just a day or two. The desire to be a positive impact on or memory of that trip is part of what motivates us. Hotel bars are also a landing point for guests on their way back in, so we get a report of their adventures while they mellow out over a nightcap.'

Meaghan Dorman, New York-based bar director at Raines Law Room and Dear Irving, as well as Raines Law Room at The William hotel and Dear Irving on Hudson at the Aliz Hotel Times Square.

• • • • • • • • • • •

'For me, opening a tiki bar in a hotel was an act of resurrection: back during tiki's golden age in the 1950s and 60s, some of the best tiki places were in hotels. The Trader Vic's chain had restaurants in Hiltons across the US and Europe; the Kon-Tiki Ports chain opened lavish, multi-million-dollar Polynesian palaces, complete with dining room waterfalls and lagoons, in Sheraton hotels; and even Marriott hotels had their own tiki chain, the Kona Kai. Being in a hotel can be a transporting experience, so being in a tiki bar inside a hotel can be doubly so.'

Jeff 'Beachbum' Berry, author, historian and owner of Latitude 29 at Bienville House Hotel in New Orleans.

• • • • • • • • • • •

'Grupo Habita, without even knowing it, invented the pool rooftop bar in 2000.

Before the Standard, Downtown LA, Soho House New York or Fasano in Rio, we had discovered a new way of drinking. It all started in Mexico City – a bar on the roof next to a pool and a great party scene. Not only did the bar at Hotel Habita, with its huge projection screen on the wall of the building across the street, change the way we partied in Mexico City, but it also inspired other hotel groups to change the way they designed and conceived nightlife. Bars went from dark and underground to outdoors, on top of buildings and around a pool. The trend has not stopped since. For us, it takes four ingredients to make a great bar: unique lighting, inventive drinks, good music and a sexy crowd. Its success has little to do with design. Our hotels are known for their great energy. We reinvent ourselves every time.'

Carlos Couturier, *managing partner at the Mexico City-based boutique hotel developer and operator, Grupo Habita.*

. . . .

'There is a sense of anonymity at a hotel bar. Even if you're somewhat of a regular travelling through a few times a year, it's certainly not your neighbourhood bar. You are who you say you are. You drink slightly differently. You're not afraid to order your favourite classic, yet off-the-beaten-path cocktail. You have confidence in your bartender. Surprisingly, having been of service to famous entertainers and politicians for many years, it's my experiences with guests whose families had history connected to Waldorf Astoria New York that stay with me the most – the more personal stories: someone whose grandparents met at the clock in the lobby on a blind date; a married couple

who met by chance at a charity ballroom event; a now-successful businessman whose initial meetings were held in the lobby because he had not yet been able to afford an office; none of these events could have happened at many other locales.'

Frank Caiafa, *author and beverage director at The Stayton Room inside Lexington Hotel, Autograph Collection, in New York, and former bar manager of Peacock Alley and La Chine at Waldorf Astoria New York.*

. . . .

'I believe that Bemelmans thrived not solely because of the success of the cocktail programme, but because internally the interpersonal energy within the room had grown into a very supportive, positive one. I believe that real hospitality begins at home, with the very people that you work alongside every day. It was my first time working with a union, which in Manhattan dictated the type of service that was provided to guests. Bemelmans was staffed with older gentlemen who had all been working there together for many years; two of them for over 50 years, one having served President Truman. It is the depth of concern and care that you show to the people you work with that I believe has allowed my teams to thrive and become successes in their own right over the years. I took care of those gents as if they were my own flesh and blood. I gave them honesty, trust and humanity, and in turn they did exactly the same for me.'

Audrey Saunders, *owner of New York's former Pegu Club and former beverage director at Bemelmans Bar.*

unique lighting

...

inventive
drinks

...

good music

...

a sexy crowd

BEHIND THE BAR

No. 12

Passion Royale

BEMELMANS BAR
AT THE CARLYLE,
NEW YORK, USA

INGREDIENTS

90 ml (3 fl oz) X-Rated Fusion
  Liqueur
Canard-Duchêne Champagne,
  to top up
¼ lime, for squeezing

METHOD

Fill a chilled Martini glass with
a handful of crushed ice and
pour in the passion fruit vodka.
Add a splash of Canard-Duchêne
Champagne and squeeze in the
lime, leaving the squeezed lime
in the cocktail to garnish.

Ludwig Bemelmans is undoubtedly best known for *Madeline*, the darling children's book series he launched in 1939, starring a fearless little red-headed protagonist. The Austrian-born author and illustrator was also quite a talented painter – in exchange for lodging, in the mid-1940s he was commissioned to cover the walls of The Carlyle hotel's new bar in playful murals. The hotel opened in 1931 and Bemelmans' balloon- and striped-umbrella-strewn paintings evoke a charmed Central Park, weaving together vignettes such as a tie-donning rabbit smoking a cigar, while providing a light-hearted juxtaposition to such Art-Deco accoutrements as the black glass and gold leaf ceiling.

Bemelmans Bar, as it was fittingly named, was unveiled in 1947. It is the only place where it's still possible for the public to take a gander at the artist's work. It's also one of the few joints where the Upper East Side feels gloriously frozen in time, with 'Vespers', 'Luxury Sidecars' and 'Whiskey Smashes' ordered over and over again by the loyal locals who, after a night of cabaret at the hotel's Café Carlyle, sink into one of the leather banquettes for a last piano-accentuated hurrah.

No. 13

Macadamia Nut Sour

BACCHUS PIANO LOUNGE
AT WEDGEWOOD HOTEL
& SPA, VANCOUVER

INGREDIENTS

40 ml (1¼ fl oz) macadamia
   nut liqueur
25 ml (¾ fl oz) freshly squeezed
   lemon juice
15 ml (½ fl oz) simple syrup
   (page 11)
1 egg white
2 dashes of Angostura bitters
1 Guinette cherry, to garnish

METHOD

Combine all the ingredients
in a cocktail shaker and dry
shake, then add ice to the shaker
and shake vigorously. Strain
into a rocks glass and garnish
with a Guinette cherry.

It was 1984 when the late Eleni Skalbania, a native of Greece, opened the Wedgewood Hotel & Spa in downtown Vancouver. Here, across from the Vancouver Art Gallery and the then-new civic hub Robson Square, dignitaries and celebrities could discreetly check in to a European-style hotel that felt as cosy as a Cotswolds' manor house. More than 35 years later, the family-run Wedgewood, with its fringed lampshades, upholstered furniture, stash of antiques and heaps of cherry wood, hasn't lost any of that enticing grace.

Bacchus Piano Lounge – the more relaxed, yet no less elegant, zone of Bacchus, the restaurant where West-Coast ingredients get the French treatment – greets visitors with a large oil painting depicting the Roman god of wine and hedonism, for whom the bar is named. During the day, the lounge's sinuous red booths are filled with patrons partaking in lavish afternoon tea. Come evening, it's the roster of classic cocktails that gets attention, sipped to the sounds of nightly live music. Martinis, such as the stand-in-for-dessert 'Red Satin Slip' with vodka, raspberry liqueur, cranberry and lime, are plentiful.

THE AMERICAS

EUROPE

53

EUROPE

When three young and audacious former school chums opened Experimental Cocktail Club in Paris in 2007, it unleashed a forward-thinking cocktail culture in a city where such glories had largely been confined to genteel hotels. Similar bars soon sprang up in London and New York before the collective expanded to hotels, including Grand Pigalle in Paris and the Henrietta in London's Covent Garden. Experimental Group now includes a Verbier chalet, a Venetian palazzo and a Menorcan finca; and it's not surprising that all of these disparate settings put the startling cocktails for which the hospitality group is known at the forefront. Contemporary concepts such as these are flowering (and welcomed) across the continent. Even London – a city with particular classic cocktail gravitas – is wide open to astonishing guests with unpredictably well-executed creations. But the proud old girls, the bars that are portals into bygone days of pocket squares, Scotch-sipping tycoons and bronzed celebrities necking on terraces, are gratefully as confident as ever.

No. 14

Hanky Panky

AMERICAN BAR
AT THE SAVOY,
LONDON, UK

Created by Ada Coleman

INGREDIENTS

45 ml (1½ fl oz) London Dry Gin
45 ml (1½ fl oz) sweet red vermouth
7.5 ml (¼ fl oz) Fernet Branca
orange twist, to garnish

METHOD

Stir all the ingredients together
in a mixing glass filled with ice.
Strain into a coupe glass and
finish with an orange twist.

One peep at the Thames Foyer, with its
gazebo and patrons sat down to afternoon tea
underneath the glass-domed atrium, and it's
clear that The Savoy – former playground for
the likes of Sarah Bernhardt, George Gershwin
and Judy Garland and the first London hotel to
feature lifts that were hydraulically operated
– is every bit as luminous as when theatrical
impresario Richard D'Oyly Carte opened the
hotel in 1889. A year later, famed hotelier
César Ritz joined him as general manager.
One of the most tempting reasons to pop
into the Edwardian-meets-Art-Deco hotel
in theatre-packed Covent Garden is the
grand-piano-shaped American Bar, going
strong since the 1890s (1904 in this location).

Drink-slinging females were a rarity in
1903, when Ada Coleman was named head
bartender, yet she held that post for over two
decades. Together with Harry Craddock, the
bartender who compiled the recipes for *The
Savoy Cocktail Book,* which published in 1930,
they moulded the American Bar's reputation.
In more recent years, bartenders like Peter
Dorelli and Erik Lorincz ensured that it was
preserved. Do try a drink from the 'Savoy
Songbook', a modern-day tribute to musicians
such as Aretha Franklin and Elvis Presley, then
order a 'White Lady' from the vintage menu.
Heightened by the pianist in the background,
it's a jolt of old-fashioned romance.

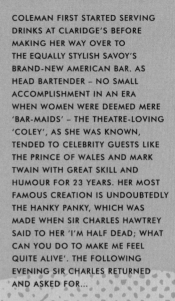

COLEMAN FIRST STARTED SERVING DRINKS AT CLARIDGE'S BEFORE MAKING HER WAY OVER TO THE EQUALLY STYLISH SAVOY'S BRAND-NEW AMERICAN BAR. AS HEAD BARTENDER – NO SMALL ACCOMPLISHMENT IN AN ERA WHEN WOMEN WERE DEEMED MERE 'BAR-MAIDS' – THE THEATRE-LOVING 'COLEY', AS SHE WAS KNOWN, TENDED TO CELEBRITY GUESTS LIKE THE PRINCE OF WALES AND MARK TWAIN WITH GREAT SKILL AND HUMOUR FOR 23 YEARS. HER MOST FAMOUS CREATION IS UNDOUBTEDLY THE HANKY PANKY, WHICH WAS MADE WHEN SIR CHARLES HAWTREY SAID TO HER 'I'M HALF DEAD; WHAT CAN YOU DO TO MAKE ME FEEL QUITE ALIVE'. THE FOLLOWING EVENING SIR CHARLES RETURNED AND ASKED FOR...

'some more of that hanky-panky'.

No. 15

White
Mouse

THE AMERICAN BAR
AT THE STAFFORD
LONDON, UK

INGREDIENTS

50 ml (1¾ fl oz) Gabriel Boudier
  Saffron Gin
25 ml (¾ fl oz) freshly squeezed
  lemon juice
15 ml (½ fl oz) Rosemary Syrup*
10 ml (⅓ fl oz) egg white
Champagne, to top up
fresh rosemary sprig, to garnish

*For the Rosemary Syrup
500 ml (17 fl oz) water
500 g (1 lb 2 oz) sugar
bunch of fresh rosemary

METHOD

For the Rosemary Syrup, combine
the water and sugar in a saucepan
and heat until the sugar dissolves.
Add the rosemary and bring to a
boil, then pour the mixture into
a sterilised glass jar and let cool.
  To make the cocktail, combine
the saffron gin, lemon juice,
rosemary syrup and egg white in
a cocktail shaker and dry shake.
Add ice to the shaker, then shake
again. Strain into a coupe glass
and top up with Champagne.
Garnish with a rosemary sprig.

Hidden away from the hubbub of Piccadilly,
the first thing one notices upon entering
The Stafford London is how desirably quiet
it is. Built in the 17th century as private
residences fit for a lord, The Stafford London
opened in 1912. Abundant in Victorian
flourishes and complete with carriage-house
accommodations where guests sleep in one-
time stables overlooking a cobbled courtyard,
it feels less like a hotel than a noble mansion.
During World War II, The Stafford London was
a stomping ground for homesick American and
Canadian officers, while its labyrinthine wine
cellars – a 1600s relic –served as an air raid
shelter.

At The American Bar, where bar manager
Benoit Provost – a fixture since 1993 – is the
debonair host, autographed photos and a
mish-mash of baseball caps, flags and model
aeroplanes dangling from the ceiling allude
to a colourful past. Nancy Wake, an Allies spy,
frequented the bar and now there's a zingy
cocktail in her honour called the 'White Mouse',
the moniker given to the stealthy Wake by
the Germans. Despite the inviting element
of kitsch, The American Bar is a class act –
a union of marble and mahogany that calls
to mind a decidedly private St James's club.

No. 16

Mulata Daisy

CONNAUGHT BAR
AT THE CONNAUGHT,
LONDON, UK

Created by Ago Perrone

INGREDIENTS

40 ml (1⅓ fl oz) Bacardi Superior rum
20 ml (⅔ fl oz) freshly squeezed
   lime juice
1 teaspoon caster (superfine) sugar
½ teaspoon fennel seeds
20 ml (⅔ fl oz) dark crème de
   cacao liqueur
10 ml (⅓ fl oz) Galliano
cacao powder, to decorate the glass

METHOD

Combine all the ingredients in
a cocktail shaker filled with ice
and shake. Decorate the rim of a
coupe glass by dipping it into the
cacao powder. Double strain the
cocktail into the decorated glass.

It's hard to resist anything served in a room designed by the late David Collins and Connaught Bar is no exception. Consider the trolley, from which a bespoke Tanqueray No 10 Martini is prepared tableside, as it roves against a background of original oak panelling enlivened by textured silver leaf and overlaid with pastel linen panels that channel Cubism. The 'Faraway Collins', a global-inspired take on the go-to quencher Tom Collins (Star of Bombay gin, sarsaparilla soda water, fresh yuzu juice, homemade eucalyptus-infused simple syrup), is equally exquisite.

The bar opened in 2008 with Ago Perrone at the helm and, mirroring its balanced interior design, it doesn't shy away from the experimental, nor does it break away from the past. How could it, when The Connaught, which opened in 1897, has such a splendid one, just like its sister properties The Berkeley and Claridge's. This Mayfair institution, at which Charles de Gaulle often lodged, telegraphs a hushed country estate; its carpeted staircase with glossy wood bannisters a highlight. Scope out the massive art collection – peppered with pieces by greats such as Louise Bourgeois and Julian Opie.

EUROPE

SPOTLIGHT:
SIGNIFICANT ARCHITECTURE
a rich architecture and design heritage only heightens a bar's ambience.
Visit these hotels for a memorable backdrop.

GOOD BONES

Four Seasons Hotel Gresham Palace Budapest, Hungary: A 1906 Art Nouveau masterpiece, originally built for the Gresham Life Assurance Company by Zsigmond Quittner and József Vágó, it retains gobs of Secessionist-style features, including Zsolnay ceramic tiles, Miksa Róth-made stained glass, wrought-iron railings and peacock gates. Admire them all before drinking a 'Smoky Forest' (mezcal, blood orange, pine) at KOLLÁZS.

The Merchant Hotel, Belfast, Northern Ireland: The old sandstone Ulster Bank building in Belfast's Cathedral Quarter is a Victorian stunner, done up in the Italianate style, with sculptures carved into its façade. Today, it's home to the Merchant Hotel, and it's blessed with intact friezes and Corinthian columns. In the Cocktail Bar, where classics such as the Bramble and Grasshopper get much-deserved play, an antique fireplace and Baccarat chandeliers remind visitors of the room's 19th-century roots.

Hotel Metropole, Brussels, Belgium: Walk through the Hotel Metropole's French Renaissance main entrance and into the column- and pillar-lined Empire-style reception hall, and the stained-glass windows and mahogany will usher you back into the 1890s. That's when French architect Alban Chambon completed the hotel, best known for Café Metropole. Here, patrons take in the Art Nouveau decor from one of the tables while drinking an easy-to-make Black Russian with vodka and coffee liqueur. Gustave Tops, one-time bartender at the hotel, is attributed with inventing the drink in 1949, in honour of the US ambassador to Luxembourg.

Delano South Beach, Miami, US: Philippe Starck's good-humoured chess set in the garden is what most Delano guests remember. But the zany designer's imprint is found throughout the hotel, including the oversized pink sofa in the lobby and the Victorian pool table balanced on curved, chunky legs. Ian Schrager opened the Delano in 1995, determined to invigorate a then seamy stretch of South Beach. Schrager might no longer be involved, but after one 'Piquant Paloma' (Don Julio tequila blanco, Ancho Reyes, grapefruit juice, agave nectar) at the pink-tinted Rose Bar, it's clear that the champion hotelier's eyebrow-raising move was yet another stylish victory.

The Dewberry Charleston, South Carolina, US: As you drink your 'Dark as Night' (Pierre Ferrand Ambre Cognac, Barolo Chinato, Austrian walnut liqueur) in the Living Room at the Dewberry Charleston, you'll expect a cigarette case to tumble out of a suit pocket and onto the ground at any given moment. The Living Room, with its books, cherry wood and radiant brass bar, truly feels tugged out of a mid-century film script – a nod to the hotel's days as the L. Mendel Rivers Federal Building (erected in 1964).

Hilton Sydney, Australia: Downstairs at the Hilton Sydney, Marble Bar is an upbeat venue that fills with locals who want to kick back with live music and an 'Autumn in New York' (tequila, apple liqueur, apple, agave, citrus). If they pay careful attention, though, they'll realise that they are also in one of the city's most breath-taking rooms. A sea of marble and cedar, it is crowned with a plastered ceiling, which – following the dismantling of the original 1893 Italian Renaissance-style bar of the same name – was refurbished and carefully re-assembled here, piece by piece, in 1968.

No. 17

La Violetera

1912 MUSEO BAR
AT THE WESTIN PALACE,
MADRID, SPAIN

INGREDIENTS

50 ml (1¾ fl oz) Belvedere vodka
30 ml (1 fl oz) Monin violet syrup
  (crème de violette will create
  a silkier texture)
20 ml (⅔ fl oz) grapefruit juice
  (pink grapefruit juice is
  a lovely alternative)
15 ml (½ fl oz) Monin blueberry
  syrup (the bar uses 20 ml/⅔ fl oz,
  but it tastes brighter with less)
fresh mint leaves, to garnish

METHOD

Combine all the ingredients in a
cocktail shaker filled with ice and
shake. Strain into an old fashioned
glass filled with crushed ice and
garnish with mint leaves.

Ernest Hemingway was an avid fan of the
Prado, arguably one of the world's most
notable museums, so when he was in Madrid
he liked to stay just across the street from it at
the Palace Hotel. Inevitably, he would follow up
those art excursions with dry Martinis downed
at the Palace Bar, which makes a cameo in his
1926 novel, *The Sun Also Rises*. Pablo Picasso
and poets such as Federico García Lorca,
who comprised the prominent Generation of
'27 group, relished the watering hole as well.

Now The Westin Palace, the hotel opened
in 1912 on once-palatial grounds at the behest
of King Alfonso XIII, who craved a splashy
modern property for the city. Its compelling
history – during the Spanish Civil War, for
example, it doubled as a makeshift hospital –
can best be appreciated from the 1912
Museo Bar (as the Palace Bar was renamed),
sipping on an effervescent 'Ginger Collins'.
Wood-panelled and dotted with sage-green
armchairs, it is akin to a library, with numerous
artefacts to peruse. Silver glasses used by
the king to toast the hotel's opening and a
letter adorned with Salvador Dalí's scribbles
all help piece together the hotel's rich
cultural heritage.

PALACE HOTEL

EUROPE

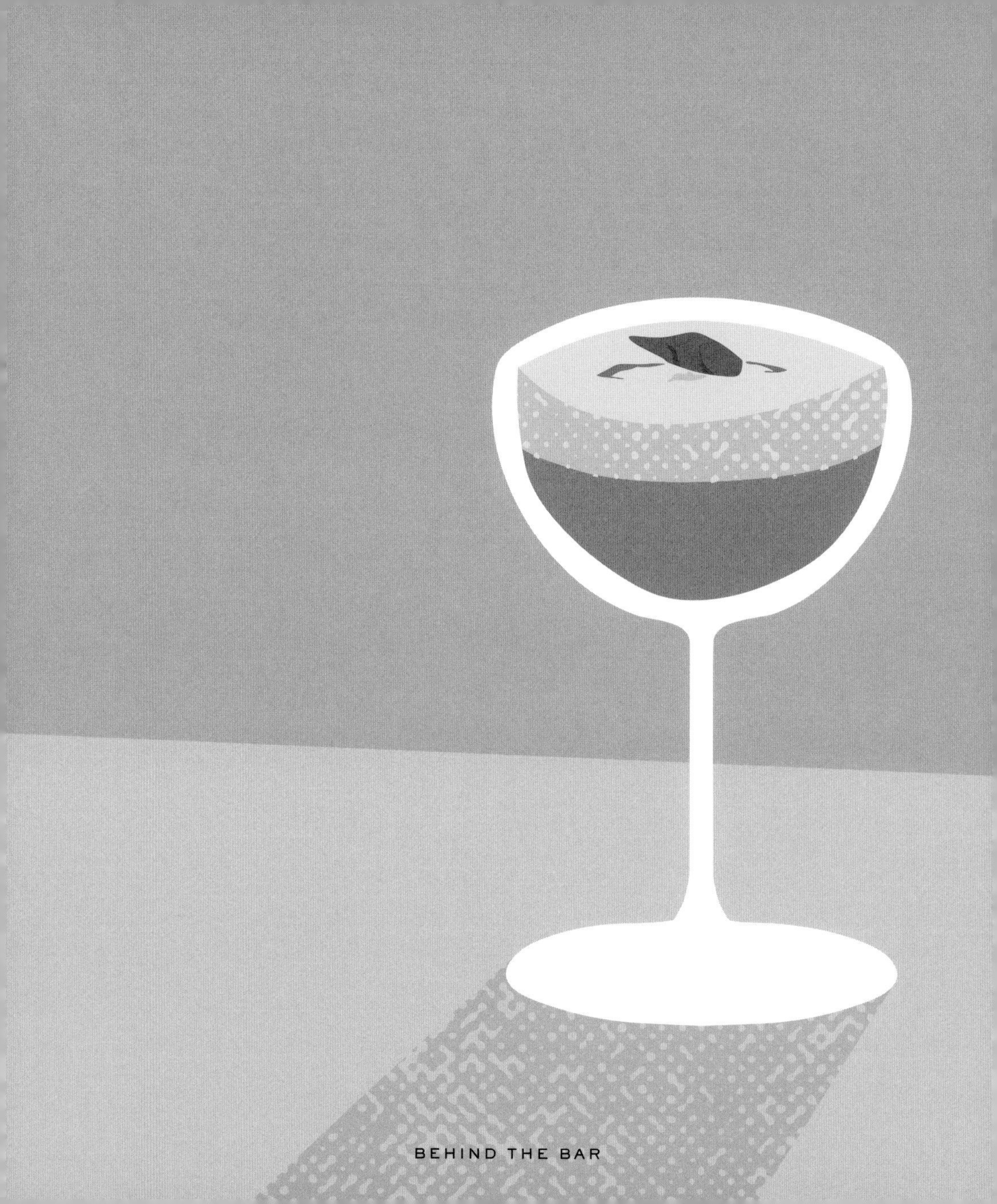

BEHIND THE BAR

No. 18

Calorosa

LE BAR AMÉRICAIN
AT HÔTEL DE PARIS
MONTE-CARLO, MONACO

Created by Ghisolfi Lorenzo

INGREDIENTS

1 chilli seed
50 ml (1¾ fl oz) Aperol
25 ml (¾ fl oz) Bombay gin
25 ml (¾ fl oz) limoncello
25 ml (¾ fl oz) freshly squeezed
  lemon juice
50 ml (1¾ fl oz) passion fruit juice
15 ml (½ fl oz) egg white
candied pepper strip (or regular
  red [bell] pepper strip), to garnish

METHOD

Crush the chilli seed in the bottom
of the cocktail shaker, then pour
in the other ingredients and dry
shake. Strain into a coupette, then
garnish the top of the drink with
a strip of pepper.

To many, Monaco is a sheer fantasy populated by royalty – a sunny enclave fuelled by grandiose wealth. A visit to this tiny French Riviera principality is therefore surprising, because, despite the onslaught of gold-encrusted surfaces and hefty bank accounts, it is more chill than haughty. Le Bar Américain, located inside the Belle Époque Hôtel de Paris Monte-Carlo, is one place that triumphantly straddles opulent and down-to-earth. The hotel, opened in 1864, underwent a massive renovation, which was completed in 2018, making way for two rambling suites that were co-designed by Prince Albert II in honour of his parents, Prince Rainier III and Princess Grace Kelly. Le Bar Américain sports a terrace that opens onto the Mediterranean Sea, but the softly lit interior is just as hypnotic, with mirrored panels, sweeping curtains and booze bottles tucked into arches all eliciting a hard-to-find retro-glam ambience. Steps away from Place du Casino, the bar is sure to have more than a few high-rollers leaning back in leather armchairs at any given time. They too will be revelling in their 'Duhamel' cocktails (Goslings rum, cider, ginger, cardamom, lime, green apple) and the sounds of live jazz.

No. 19

Meurice Millennium

BAR 228 AT LE MEURICE, PARIS, FRANCE

Created by William Oliveri

INGREDIENTS

20 ml (⅔ fl oz) Cointreau
10 ml (⅓ fl oz) crème de rose liqueur
130 ml (4⅓ fl oz) rosé Champagne
pared strip of orange zest,
to garnish

METHOD

Pour the Cointreau and crème de rose into a Champagne flute. Top off with the Champagne and garnish with orange zest.

After a spell on Rue Saint-Honoré, Le Meurice moved over to Rue de Rivoli in 1835, wooing well-to-do British tourists with a premier location across from the Tuileries Garden and underneath a tasteful row of arcades. With sizable apartments, smoking and reading rooms, and private dinners then on offer, it's no wonder Le Meurice became a favourite among royalty – beginning with Queen Victoria's visit in 1855. The first hotel in Paris to flaunt telephones and baths in every guest room, Le Meurice retains a ritzy, 19th-century tone, starting in the gilded lobby. Contemporised with a frosted mirror and updated Louis XVI-style chairs inspired by hotel regular Salvador Dalí, it leads to the low-lit Bar 228.

It's not the original 1936 lair, and eccentric designer Philippe Starck has spruced up the joint with pink copper, brass and stainless steel, but the dreamy painted ceiling and early 20th-century fresco panels by Alexandre Claude Louis Lavalley plunge you back to a time when guests such as Rudyard Kipling and Ginger Rogers might have sipped nightcaps at the hotel.

William Oliveri manned the bar at Le Meurice for decades, plying guests with bubbly cocktails and dry Martinis until he retired. The next generation of bartenders, thankfully, continue to intensify the impression that you are indeed somewhere special. When the hotel reopened in 2000 after a lustrous renovation, Oliveri's celebratory cocktail went on the menu. It's been clamoured for ever since.

EUROPE

BAR HEMINGWAY
PARIS, FRANCE

BEHIND THE BAR

No. 20

The Serendipity

BAR HEMINGWAY
AT RITZ PARIS,
FRANCE

Created by Colin Field

INGREDIENTS

1 fresh mint sprig
20 ml (⅔ fl oz) Calvados
30 ml (1 fl oz) apple juice
Champagne (the bar uses its
   own Ritz Réserve Brut Barons
   de Rothschild), to top up

METHOD

Add the mint sprig to a highball
glass filled with ice, then pour
in the Calvados and apple juice.
Top up with Champagne.

There are only 35 seats at Bar Hemingway and night after night there are eager imbibers who contentedly wait to settle into one of them. Named for the peripatetic author who was so enamoured with the Ritz bar that he supposedly tried to rescue it from the Germans in 1944, then knocked back a staggering 51 dry Martinis in celebration of Paris's liberation, Bar Hemingway might just be the globe's most well-known hotel bar. The Ritz opened on Place Vendôme in 1898, and F. Scott Fitzgerald and Cole Porter drank here well before Bar Hemingway's modern unveiling in 1994. History, magnified by old photographs and antiques such as a typewriter, gramophone and boxing gloves strewn about, certainly appeals to the curious queues, but the lure of the intimate room extends to the clubby blend of oak and pine-green carpeting, as well as the white-jacketed barmen. Colin Field – the most revered of them – has made the bar his home since it re-opened, dreaming up cocktails like the 'Clean Dirty Martini' along the way. That guests can drink one alongside petite hot dogs, the bar snack of choice, underscores how extravagance is best when there's a dash of the amusing.

A BAR CRAWL THROUGH LONDON

London is arguably home to the world's best hotel bars. Other than the three must-visit establishments at The Connaught, The Savoy and The Stafford London (see pages 60, 56 and 58), there are plenty of other remarkable spots throughout the city for a welcome 'Old Fashioned' respite, including these:

• • • • • • • • • • • •

Artesian at The Langham, London: Directly across from BBC Broadcasting House in Marylebone, The Langham, London opened in 1865. During World War II, the hotel became the stomping ground for American reporters. Named for the 111-metre- (365-feet-) deep well underneath the hotel, which once supplied fresh water for its stylish guests, Artesian's David Collins' interior mixes Victorian-era romance with Far-East intrigue. Menu concepts are always in flux, so look out for thematic concoctions such as the 'minimalist' hybrids of St-Germain liqueur and carrot or Cognac and green coffee.

• • • • • • • • • • •

The Coral Room at The Bloomsbury Hotel: With all the oomph of a 1920s grand Euro café, The Coral Room, completed by Martin Brudnizki in 2017, is a chic newcomer to the hotel bar scene. Drink a 'May Day Spritz' (Monkey 47 gin, Italicus Rosolio di Bergamotto, apricot honey water, Empirical Spirits Fallen Pony and Ridgeview Bloomsbury sparkling wine) against marble, Murano glass and walls painted in the bar's namesake hue. For the second tipple, head downstairs to The Bloomsbury Club Bar. The Bloomsbury Group surely would have been eager to partake of philosophical discussions in this brooding leather-and-wood room or on the adjoining, twinkling terrace.

• • • • • • • • • • •

DUKES Bar at DUKES LONDON: No one can prove that James Bond scribe Ian Fleming was struck with inspiration for 007's famous 'shaken, not stirred' motto while drinking at DUKES Bar, as some claim, but what is certain is that the Martini acquired a whole new level of cachet at this very bar in the 1980s. That's when venerated bartender Salvatore Calabrese started working at the hotel dating from 1908 and introduced captivated clientele to his and Gilberto Preti's 'direct Martini', a rendition of the drink that shuns ice for frozen gin. After Calabrese and Preti came Alessandro Palazzi, who – in his suave white jacket – still makes his Martinis from a mobile rosewood trolley in the same fashion. The chilled glass is first rinsed with dry vermouth made in collaboration with local distillery Sacred Spirits, the frozen gin (or vodka) is added and then the cocktail is simply finished with Palazzi's own twist: an aromatic Amalfi-Coast lemon zest. These Martinis are so potent that only two of them can be served to any one guest.

• • • • • • • • • • •

George's Bar at St Pancras Renaissance Hotel London: There is no more fashionable send-off to the Paris-bound Eurostar than a cocktail at the moody burgundy-and-brass George's Bar – designed by David Collins Studio in 2018. Directly inside St Pancras International Station, this haunt adjacent to Marcus Wareing's Gilbert Scott restaurant is an ode to George Gilbert Scott, the architect who designed this very building as the Midland Grand Hotel, a fancy 19th-century railway bolthole. With all those passengers running to and from trains, George's is certainly a magnet for people-watching while sipping an 'Amber Embers' (Lapsang Souchong tea-infused Scotch, Martini Rosso, apricot, lemon, smoke) underneath the ceiling's cluster of extraordinary original bells, but it's hard to take your eyes off the friezes and fringed lamps.

• • • • • • • • • • • •

Punch Room at The London EDITION: Although additional Punch Room locations have now sprouted in the Barcelona and Shanghai incarnations of Ian Schrager and Marriott International's EDITION Hotels, the concept first kicked off in 2013, at the EDITION London in Fitzrovia. The original, with its fumed oak bar and surreptitiously drawn blinds straight out of a 19th-century gentlemen's club, remains the city's choice locale for punches that commingle ingredients such as Wild Turkey rye, Martini bitters, Martini Rubino, hibiscus tea and red (bell) pepper syrup, or a comforting cold-weather 'Grog' (Plantation OFTD rum, lime juice, grapefruit sherbet, Cornish Manuka tea, nutmeg).

• • • • • • • • • • • •

Scarfes Bar at Rosewood London: English cartoonist and illustrator Gerald Scarfe, who created the promo video for Pink Floyd's 'Another Brick in the Wall (part 2)', lent his name and his artistic prowess to this bar at the Rosewood London when it opened on High Holborn in 2013. Bearing the signature

upbeat-clubby imprint of designer Martin Brudnizki, the magnetic room is graced with Scarfe's caricatures of well-known Brits such as Mick Jagger and Margaret Thatcher. Look out for changing Scarfe-illustrated menus that may nod to different musical genres such as jazz and classical with the 'Crescent City Crusta' (Rémy Martin 1738, pandan, banana vinegar, unripe grape) and 'Curtain Call' (Roe & Co Irish whiskey, clarified carob, hazelnut and mint, fortified wine, liquorice), respectively.

London is arguably home to the world's best hotel bars.

No. 21

St Moritzino

RENAISSANCE BAR
AT BADRUTT'S PALACE,
ST MORITZ, SWITZERLAND

Created by Mario da Como

INGREDIENTS

40 ml (1¼ fl oz) Russian Standard
   Original vodka
30 ml (1 fl oz) Cointreau
20 ml (⅔ fl oz) freshly squeezed
   lemon juice
10 ml (⅓ fl oz) Orgeat Fabbri
   or Monin almond syrup

METHOD

Shake all the ingredients in a
cocktail shaker filled with ice,
then strain into a Martini glass.

Every winter, the Patek-Philippe-donning elite descend upon the Swiss resort town of St Moritz to hit the slopes. They have Johannes Badrutt to thank for this cold-weather ritual, for in the 1860s he made a bet with British guests at his Kulm Hotel that if they didn't love staying there in the coldest months, too, he would foot the bill of their return visit. By the time Johannes' son, Caspar, opened the Palace – a hotel of his own – in 1896, St Moritz was a hotbed of bobsleds and toboggans. Still, alpine tourism doesn't thrive on sports alone. Thrill-seekers also came to Badrutt's Palace, then, as they do now, for the eddy of après-ski soirees.

Back in the 1960s, those who hankered for a less raucous environment than the basement discotheque (one of the first in Switzerland), went to the Renaissance Bar instead. There, they likely encountered barkeep Mario da Como, who arrived in 1963 and stayed for more than 40 years. Maybe they even spotted Alfred Hitchcock, who spent myriad holidays at the Palace, Audrey Hepburn or Marlene Dietrich. Renaissance Bar carries on, and sitting by the crackling fireplace, a cigar paired with one of the classic libations from the A–Z 'Cocktail Library', is amped chalet sipping at its best.

Long-time barman Mario da Como no longer holds court at Badrutt's Palace, but his jovial presence is still felt at the Renaissance Bar, playfully dubbed 'Mario's Bar'. His bright 'St Moritzino', first spawned in 1972 from an embargoed bottle of South African rum gifted to the hotel's then-owner Andrea Badrutt, has since metamorphised into a vodka tipple. It remains a favourite among the hotel's discriminating clientele.

BADRUTT'S PALACE,
ST MORITZ, SWITZERLAND

No. 22

Bellini

BAR LONGHI AT
THE GRITTI PALACE,
VENICE, ITALY

*Created by Giuseppe Cipriani,
Harry's Bar*

INGREDIENTS

30 ml (1 fl oz) peach purée
90 ml (3 fl oz) chilled prosecco

METHOD

Gently stir the ingredients
directly in a coupe glass.

No matter how many times they gape at it, the straight-out-of-a-fable Grand Canal buoys visitors to Venice, especially if it's seen from the amorous environs of The Gritti Palace. Built in the 15th century by the Pisani family, this gothic palazzo, converted into a hotel in 1895, was once the residence of the 16th-century Doge Andrea Gritti. VIPs such as W. Somerset Maugham, Elizabeth Taylor and Greta Garbo were all devotees of the enchanting property, and they'd certainly still be pleased to wake up to the silk damask walls. With its terrazzo-etched mirrors and Murano-glass chandeliers, Bar Longhi, yet another of Hemingway's preferred hide-outs, has the pristine aura of an oil painting come to life. In the summer, the seat that everyone wants, though, is on Riva Lounge terrace, facing Basilica di Santa Maria della Salute with a 'Bellini' (the uplifting drink was invented by Giuseppe Cipriani at Harry's Bar, a few minutes' walk away) or a 'Basil-ica' (Old Tom gin, lemon juice, St-Germain liqueur, basil, orange bitters). As the sun sets, the water gleams, and you never want to leave the city.

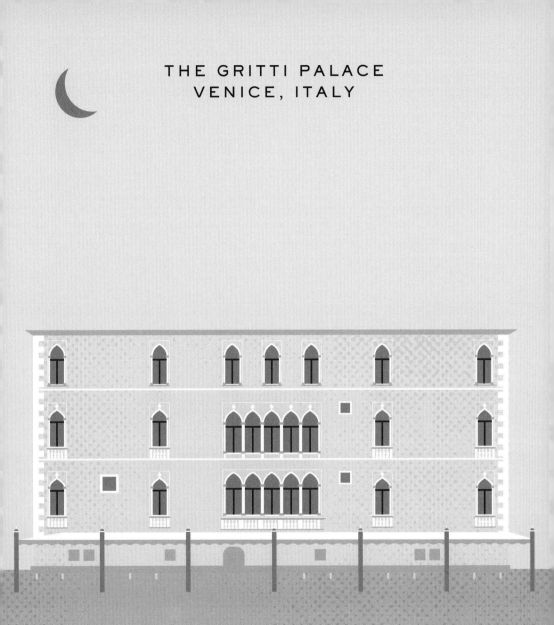

THE GRITTI PALACE
VENICE, ITALY

BEHIND THE BAR

No. 23

Apricot Sour

STRAVINSKIJ BAR
AT HOTEL DE RUSSIE,
ROME, ITALY

*Created by Paolo Danini
and Barbara Simmi*

INGREDIENTS

25 ml (¾ fl oz) The Glenlivet Founder's
  Reserve
35 ml (1¼ fl oz) apricot distillate
  (Stravinskij Bar uses Capovilla
  Distillato di Albicocche from Vesuvio)
12 ml (1 scant tablespoon) vanilla syrup
2 teaspoons organic apricot jam (jelly)
20 ml (⅔ fl oz) freshly squeezed
  lemon juice
2 dashes of Angostura bitters,
  to garnish
fresh apricot wedge, to garnish

METHOD

Shake all the ingredients in a cocktail
shaker filled with ice, then strain back
into an empty shaker. Dry shake, then
double strain into a chilled coupe glass.
Garnish with a few drops of Angostura
bitters and the apricot wedge affixed
to garnish.

Piazza del Popolo, one of Rome's most
remarkable squares, was spiffed up in the
1820s by architect Giuseppe Valadier. Steps
from it, he completed a building during the
same time period that became a hotel,
gaining the favour of Russian nobility and
Jean Cocteau, and it eventually morphed into
the headquarters of a top Italian television
station. In 2000, Sir Rocco Forte swooped
it up and added it to his hotel collection and
soon a stay at Hotel de Russie was as coveted
as those at Eternal City legends the Eden and
Hassler.

Much of its mystique comes from the
terraced gardens, where guests eat *cacio e
pepe* ravioli surrounded by roses and orange
trees. Stravinskij Bar is an equally splendorous
al fresco enterprise, with patrons taking to
the courtyard and sitting down under shady
umbrellas to inventive aperitivo-hour tipples
such as a Bloody Mary that swaps tomato
juice for perky carrot, and the 'Modern Fizzy',
a highball pairing saffron-infused Cognac and
rum with honey-black peppercorn syrup
and cardamom liqueur. In gloomy weather,
la dolce vita persists; dotted with statuary,
the interior of Stravinskij Bar is an upscale
ode to ancient Rome.

BEHIND THE BAR

No. 24

Tesoro

PULITZER'S BAR
AT PULITZER
AMSTERDAM,
THE NETHERLANDS

INGREDIENTS

50 ml (1¾ fl oz) Ron Zacapa
   23 rum
20 ml (⅔ fl oz) Taylor's
   10-Year-Old tawny port
10 ml (⅓ fl oz) Grand Marnier
3 dashes of Aphrodite bitters
1 barspoon maple syrup
1 strip of orange zest, to garnish

METHOD

Combine all the ingredients
in a mixing glass, then add ice
cubes and stir for 20 seconds.
Strain into a chilled rocks glass
filled with ice cubes and add
the orange zest to garnish.

By 1960, the gloriously narrow 17th-
and 18th-century canal houses in which
Amsterdam merchants and aristocrats
once cavorted had sadly deteriorated.
Peter Pulitzer, the visionary grandson of the
Hungarian-born, American newspaper titan
Joseph Pulitzer, saw potential in reviving
them and snatched up 12 to transform into
a five-star hotel with an unlikely partner:
the modest American motel and restaurant
chain, Howard Johnson's. Eventually, the
maze of homes and warehouses between
the Keizersgracht and Prinsengracht canals
grew to 25. Several owners later, the Pulitzer –
original wood beams intact – was reinvented
in 2016. Fortunately, this time around there
was Pulitzer's Bar, a purple-tinged respite for
fireside conversations, with plush armchairs
that comfort after an exhausting day of
sightseeing (the hotel's prime Nine Streets
location means many museums are within
walking distance) and imaginatively themed
cocktail menus that celebrate, say, Agatha
Christie's *Murder on the Orient Express* with
cocktails like 'The Doctor' (whisky, whey,
sherry and genmaicha tea). Catch a glimpse
of the golden, geometric-patterned bar
sparkling against the dark walls, and it feels
like you've stepped inside one of Rembrandt's
moody paintings.

At Pulitzer's Bar, Tesoro is served aged,
but it is also satisfyingly heady in its *à-la-
minute* form.

SINGLE-MINDED

Many hotel bars, just by the very nature of their energetic, public locations, seem to warmly welcome folks right into the lobby. They tend to be inclusive spaces, and no matter who you are and no matter what part of the globe you might be visiting from, there is something on the menu that is bound to strike your fancy and put you at ease, whether it's a glass of rosé or a complicated tequila drink. But this is not always the case. Some hotel bars have strong personalities and offer sharply defined experiences with a specific roster of cocktails to match. These places are destinations fuelled by a singular vision – usually reflected in the menu or sometimes the design – and they aren't meant to entertain the mainstream masses. Hotel bars can inhabit an out-of-the-ordinary world, and that is what these particular bars do.

Take **Fragrances** at the **Ritz-Carlton, Berlin**. Guests who want to spend the evening knocking back a few Martinis on Potsdamer Platz should walk over to the lobby's Curtain Club instead of coming here, because this aromatic haven is meant for guests who want to turn their night into an interactive sensory journey. Instead of being handed a classic menu, they will whiff their way through an artfully curated wall of fragrances, seeing the corresponding liquor bottles beckon to them from bell jars. Barkeeps here know exactly how to translate a perfume's olfactory profile to cocktail form. Aventure – a nod to Berlin's own Frau Tonis Parfum scent – is a delicate mix of rose lemonade, Yamagata Masamune sake, verjus, bergamot, orange blossom water grenadine and an earthy syrup of vanilla, vetiver, ylang-ylang, patchouli and

sandalwood. The 'Vaara', which references the Penhaligon's potion of the same name, combines pear purée with saffron-infused Zacapa 23 rum, Bulleit bourbon, rosewater and vanilla-honey-tonka-bean syrup.

If you like the idea of planning an outing to an alluring niche bar, consider these:

Black Angel's Bar, Hotel U Prince, Prague, Czech Republic: Close to the medieval Prague Astronomical Clock, that tourist favourite on Old Town Square, is Black Angel's Bar. Hidden underneath the Hotel U Prince, it's essentially a classy cave with 1930s speakeasy leanings. Come drink a 'From Dust Till Foam' (gin, lemon, Aperol, fresh grapefruit juice, elderflower foam) or the pleasant, pretty 'Concord' (gin, dry vermouth, strawberry syrup) – both cocktails that honour the early 20th-century Czech bartender Alois Krcha – amid the soaring arches.

· · · · · · · · · · · ·

The Chandelier, The Cosmopolitan of Las Vegas, US: Hotel bars on the Las Vegas Strip are on completely different turf than their brethren. The city has considerably upped the quality of its beverage programmes through the years, led by bartenders such as the Chandelier's Mariena Mercer Boarini, yet bars are still showy and theatrical – exactly how they need to be (and, when in Vegas, how you want them to be) in order to capture the fleeting attention of restless tourists meandering across the casino floor. The Chandelier, originally designed by Rockwell Group, is comprised of three different bars, all situated within a gleaming, tri-level structure sheathed in undulating string and crystal. You're either sitting at the bottom of the Chandelier with a 'Whiskey Business' (Knob Creek bourbon, Amaro di Angostura, Amaro Meletti, 'old time rock 'n' roll' syrup); tucked inside it sipping an 'Evil Twin' (Don Julio Anejo tequila, Laird's apple brandy, Allspice Dram, Zirbenz pine liqueur, smoked maple syrup); or at the very top, trying the Mule-inspired 'Finishing School' (CÎROC Red Berry vodka, lemon, strawberry-rhubarb rose syrup, ginger beer, plum bitters).

· · · · · · · · · · · ·

The Milk Room, Chicago Athletic Association, Chicago, US: There are only eight stools at this bar on the second floor of the Chicago Athletic Association hotel, and the booze geeks who don't flinch at the hefty prices must reserve in advance. Here, bar-goers are wooed by an ever-changing stock of rare spirits such as a Very Old Fitzgerald bourbon bottled in bond from 1945–53, or a 1978 Delord Bas-Armagnac. When a bottle of 1970s Tarragona Chartreuse graces the eclectic collection, the bartender will be happy to let it sing in a truly retro 'Last Word'.

· · · · · · · · · · · ·

Tonga Room & Hurricane Bar, Fairmont San Francisco, US: In 1945, a Metro-Goldwyn-Mayer set designer was tasked with reimagining the Fairmont San Francisco's one-time pool into a lagoon and floating stage. The occasion was the opening of the Tonga Room & Hurricane Bar, a tiki paradise that embodied the post-World-War-II fascination with the Polynesian idyll. Dancing on the floor fashioned from the remains of S.S. Forester, a schooner that darted between San Francisco

and the South Seas, pausing only for sips of Don the Beachcomber's 1934 'Zombie', was all the reassurance folks needed that a better life was indeed around the bend. Overlook the cloying cocktails – you're here because the thatched roofs and tropical storms, replete with lightning and rain falling from the ceiling above the lagoon, are an illusion you're not ready to shatter.

destinations fuelled
by a singular vision

...

interactive sensory
journey

...

an allusion you're not
ready to shatter

No. 25

Juniper/ Beetroot/ Pineapple Cocktail

BAR AM STEINPLATZ
AT HOTEL AM STEINPLATZ,
BERLIN, GERMANY

INGREDIENTS

40 ml (1⅓ fl oz) Freimeister
   Doppelwacholder juniper spirit
50 ml (1¾ fl oz) Faude beetroot
   (beet) spirit
20 ml (⅔ fl oz) freshly squeezed
   lemon juice or lemon-infused water
15 ml (½ fl oz) Pineapple Syrup*
 2 drops of mint oil

*For the Pineapple Syrup:
500 ml (17 fl oz) simple syrup
   (page 11)
5 ml (1 teaspoon) pineapple essence

METHOD

For the Pineapple Syrup, combine
the simple syrup and pineapple
essence in a mixing glass.
   For the cocktail, stir all the
ingredients together in a separate
mixing glass filled with ice, then
double strain into a Nick & Nora
glass. Finish with a couple of drops
of the mint oil.

Hotel am Steinplatz opened in Berlin's swanky
Charlottenburg neighbourhood in 1913 – an
Art-Nouveau marvel that was the handiwork
of Jugendstil architect August Endell, who
designed the city's Hackesche Höfe courtyard
complex. After a restoration in 2013, the
olive-green-hued building, festooned
with geometric decorative elements, still
stands out, encouraging passersby to walk
underneath the entry's ornamental canopy
into a world that once tantalised the likes
of Vladimir Nabokov and Romy Schneider.
   The basement bar – a 1950s smash with
actors and artists – is long gone. In its place
is ground-level Bar am Steinplatz, where the
Art-Deco atmosphere, a melange of marble
and leather – black and cream – is reason
enough to pull up a stool. At first, gin lovers
might be chagrined to discover not even one
bottle of their favourite spirit skulks on the
shelves. Then, they peer at the cocktail menu,
cleverly illustrated so that each drink's taste
profile is in the limelight, and they realise
they are actually quite pleased to try one –
all of them clear, all of them served in Nick &
Nora glasses, and spun from a brazen mix of
ingredients such as pisco, kaffir, blackcurrant
and rice.

No. 26

Little Match Girl

NIMB BAR AT NIMB HOTEL,
COPENHAGEN, DENMARK

Created by António Saldanha de Oliveira

INGREDIENTS

50 ml (1¾ fl oz) Don Julio Añejo
   Tequila
10 ml (⅓ fl oz) Graham's ruby port
   or tawny port
10 ml (⅓ fl oz) Lillet Rouge
10 ml (⅓ fl oz) simple syrup
   (page 11) (2 parts sugar to
   1 part water)
2 large pieces of pared grapefruit
   or orange zest
2 large slices of galangal
   or root ginger

METHOD

Combine the liquid ingredients
in a small saucepan and place
over a low heat. Add the grapefruit
or orange zests and the galangal
or ginger slices to the mixture,
then cover with the lid and simmer
for 3–5 minutes. Strain into a mug
to serve.

Tivoli Gardens, providing merriment to
Copenhageners since 1843, is one of the
world's oldest amusement parks, and Nimb
Hotel is serendipitously plopped in the centre
of this joyful setting. When it first opened in
1909, inside a fantastical Moorish palace,
Nimb was a buzzing bazaar restaurant, named
for the same hospitable owners who had
popularised Denmark's now-ubiquitous, open-
faced rye-bread sandwiches. By 1930, the
Danish National Broadcasting Company was
recording live from Nimb, making it
a bastion of contemporary dance music.
Since 2008, Nimb has taken the form of a
soothing Nordic-style boutique hotel, with
balcony suites, a pool the shade of the
fictional Emerald City gracing the rooftop
terrace, and multiple restaurants that add
another layer to its gastronomic history.

Nimb Bar, in what was the old ballroom,
bristles with sophistication – a muted space
that allows the birch-wood-burning fireplace,
original lost-then-found crystal chandeliers
and grand piano to take centre stage. After
a day on the Ferris wheel and the animal-
bedecked carousel, Nimb Bar's afternoon tea
or blissful cocktails, such as the summery
'Little Mermaid' (Absolut Elyx vodka, lychee,
lime cordial, spirulina, coconut water and
cucumber), confirm that the fairytale need
not end here.

Little Match Girl is an elevated hot toddy,
which is wonderfully warming on those frosty-
day forays through Tivoli Gardens. Ideally it
is made with a Viennese coffee maker, but
a stovetop coffee pot or a saucepan over a
low heat, covered with a lid, will work just as
well. This recipe makes one cocktail, but it is
best served for groups of two or more; simply
multiply the ingredients accordingly.

NIMB HOTEL
COPENHAGEN, DENMARK

EUROPE

No. 27

Beautiful, Amore, Gasp

THIEF BAR AT THE THIEF,
OSLO, NORWAY

Created by Felice Capasso

INGREDIENTS

30 ml (1 fl oz) Absolut Elyx vodka
15 ml (½ fl oz) Cocchi Americano vermouth
10 ml (⅓ fl oz) white crème de cacao
10 ml (⅓ fl oz) freshly squeezed lemon juice
5 ml (1 teaspoon) Salted Pedro Ximénez Syrup*
1 ice ball, to serve (you can use a silicone mould to make these)
white chocolate shard or disc**, to garnish

For the Salted Pedro Ximénez Syrup (makes 750 ml/25 fl oz):
750 ml (25 fl oz) Pedro Ximénez Lustau sherry
350 g (12 oz) sugar
25 g (¾ oz) salt

**Former bar manager Capasso used an ornate moulded disc of white chocolate decorated with swirls of coloured chocolate to garnish this cocktail, but you can use any white chocolate of your choice.*

METHOD

For the Salted Pedro Ximénez Syrup, combine the sherry and sugar in a saucepan and gently heat for 10–15 minutes until the sugar has dissolved. Remove from the heat and stir in the salt until fully dissolved. Chill until needed.

To make the cocktail, combine all the ingredients in a cocktail shaker filled with ice and shake. Strain into a coupe glass (the bar uses an Elyx copper coupette) filled with an ice ball. Serve garnished with white chocolate.

When discussing Scandinavia's robust art and design scenes, cities like Copenhagen, Stockholm and Helsinki tend to get the lion's share of attention. Oslo should also be a part of that conversation. For example, The Astrup Fearnley Museum of Modern Art, designed by Renzo Piano, is a champion of Norwegian and international contemporary art and is located on Tjuvholmen, a renewed island that once swarmed with bandits and ladies of the night.

Adjacent to the museum is The Thief, a hotel that debuted in 2013 with gold-accented guest rooms that take cues from Riva yachts. Amplified through floor-to-ceiling windows, the views of the canals and the Oslo Fjord are a mighty visual alone, but The Thief bolsters this natural backdrop with its own permanent artwork collection, as well as selections borrowed from its prominent neighbour and collaborator.

Thief Bar, which subtly recalls a gallery with liquor bottles, books and objects all confidently displayed inside warmly illuminated shelves, deepens the strong relationship with the arts through its menu. Cerebral cocktails, in dialogue with such works as Damien Hirst's *God Alone Knows* and *Beautiful, amore, gasp, eyes going into the top of the head and fluttering painting*, are meant to arouse a contemplative state. It comes easily when seated in a velvety chair by the fireplace.

No. 28

Million
Red Roses

LOBBY BAR AT BELMOND
GRAND HOTEL EUROPE,
ST PETERSBURG, RUSSIA

INGREDIENTS

40 ml (1¼ fl oz) Russian Standard
  Platinum vodka
100 ml (3½ fl oz) grapefruit juice
40 ml (1¼ fl oz) honey syrup (1 part
  honey to 2 parts water)
100 ml (3½ fl oz) sparkling wine
aspidistra leaf and rose petals
  (optional), to garnish

METHOD

Combine the vodka, grapefruit
juice and syrup in a cocktail shaker
filled with ice and shake well.
Strain into a chilled wine glass
with a few ice cubes at the bottom.
Add the sparkling wine and stir.

The bar fancifully garnishes this
drink with aspidistra leaf and rose
petals, but it's also lovely in its
unadorned state.

Past the Ludwig Fontana-designed neo-classical façade of Belmond Grand Hotel Europe, the barrage of marble and gilt carries one back to tsarist 1875, when the property opened as Grand Hotel d'Europe. Dostoevsky came around often, Tchaikovsky honeymooned here, and the enigmatic monk Rasputin, from behind drawn curtains, dined with politicians and paramours alike in an upstairs alcove at L'Europe, the restaurant that when it opened in 1905 was lit by never-before-seen-in-St-Petersburg electric bulbs.

By turns a post-Soviet Revolution orphanage and a hospital for the Leningrad front during the early-1940s siege, the hotel is once again a shimmering Art Nouveau palace, complete with a vodka sommelier and caviar brunches befitting of the antique-laden suites such as the winter garden-accentuated 'Lidval' and the jewel-toned 'Fabergé'. In the Lobby Bar, restored stucco and tiled mantelpieces contrast with the bar crafted from smooth, icy alabaster marble and black granite. Spring for the 'Anna Akhmatova' (gin, elderflower liqueur, Lillet Blanc, dry vermouth), named for the great 20th-century Russian poet, and taste the good imperial life.

For a drier, less tart version of the Million Red Roses, then reduce the measurements to 50 ml (1¾ fl oz) of grapefruit juice and 30 ml (1 oz) of honey syrup.

EUROPE

MR LYAN!

Ryan Chetiyawardana, better known as Mr Lyan in cocktail circles, has been breaking the rules since 2013, when he opened White Lyan in London's Hoxton neighbourhood. A daring experiment in sustainability, the bar served pre-made libations devoid of fruit and ice. A year later, he unveiled Dandelyan in the Tom Dixon-designed Mondrian London hotel – now Sea Containers London – overlooking the Thames, and the accolades quickly poured in for its 'Modern Botany' menus. The green marble bar is the same and boozy afternoon tea is still on offer, but Dandelyan is no more. Instead there is Lyaness, a new Mr Lyan concept, joining his London restaurant Cub and all-day bar Super Lyan inside the Kimpton De Witt Amsterdam hotel, that dissects just seven ingredients, including vegan honey and a signature tea blend. His latest venture is Silver Lyan, which is inside yet another hotel, Riggs Washington DC. Here, Mr Lyan weighs in.

On the Endurance of Hotel Bars
'I think the best hotel bars have integrated themselves into their setting, and into the community. There is a balance that can come from these bigger projects that means they can imbed themselves into the scene in a much more open way, and that allows for the longevity.'

On Dandeylan's Triumphs
'We always said we wanted to challenge the model of a hotel bar. We wanted to integrate into the building, but not conform to the hotel bar model. There were lots of iconic hotel bars, particularly in London, but we wanted something to complement that,

and something that felt honest to us. We took a lot of the small bar sensibilities and tried to find a way to marry them with the glamorous setting of Sea Containers hotel. We took the fact that the hotel wanted to be democratic and welcoming to all – a value mirrored in what we do – and we created something that played to this, but from the point of view of innovation and being a destination. Like with Hoxton, Southbank was a destination, and lacking many great food and drink options at the time, so we created something that felt really welcoming, but was unique to act as a draw. We described it as a "neighbourhood bar in a five-star setting".'

On Forging a New Identity
'It was about playing to honesty and borrowing from our background and history. White Lyan set the tone for what we have wanted to do as a business – find new, welcoming and exciting ways to help people gather – and everything has stemmed back to this. Lyaness is very much born of the things we love, and the things we want to change in the landscape of food.'

On the Difference Between Hotel Bars and Other Kinds
'Hotel bars are much more open. They cater to every crowd and every eventuality. Independent bars can, of course, take these ideals on, but they also have the difference in being able to be more specific, niche and nuanced, so a hotel bar has a brilliant grounding in something familiar. The best will try to evolve this definition though.'

THE
MIDDLE EAST/
AFRICA/
SOUTH ASIA/
ASIA

99

THE MIDDLE EAST/ AFRICA/ SOUTH ASIA/ ASIA

Soho House, the petite empire of hotels and private members' clubs formed by Nick Jones in 1995, unveiled its Istanbul digs in 2015. The city's arts-and-media types came running to this former palazzo in Beyoğlu, holing up at the Club to drink in a dramatic room covered in marble, rosewood and original frescoes. For a region where alcohol is largely *verboten*, Middle Eastern hotel bars do a fine job of transporting their guests, even if it's through an inspired mocktail that doesn't require booze to hold interest. Further east, India has rapidly contemporised, and its bars have not been left behind. Waterlogged Maldives and Mauritius, increasingly visited for their sunny seclusion and outdoor antics, also don't skimp on their hotel bars – as if they could be anything less than radiant when facing the Indian Ocean. Decades ago, this region was cloaked in mystery and hailed as 'exotic'; sit in a hotel's citrus-scented garden and you might just feel the same.

INGREDIENTS

45 ml (1½ fl oz) Date-Infused VS Cognac*
15 ml (½ fl oz) Pineapple Coconut
  Simple Syrup**
15 ml (½ fl oz) unsweetened coconut milk
15 ml (½ fl oz) cold-brew espresso-
  blend coffee (Marshall uses Trader Joe's
  Cold-Brew Coffee, Nitrogen-Infused
  with Espresso)
freshly grated coconut, to garnish

* *For the Date-Infused VS Cognac*
  (makes 750 ml/25 fl oz):
3 large dates, sliced
750 ml (25 fl oz) VS Cognac

** *For the Pineapple Coconut Simple Syrup*
  (makes 250ml/8½ fl oz):
125 ml (4 fl oz) fresh pineapple juice
225 g (8 oz) coconut sugar

METHOD

For the Date-Infused VS Cognac, add
the sliced dates to a large non-reactive
container and then muddle gently. Pour
over the Cognac and stir. Let sit for 6–
8 hours, or longer depending on desired
intensity. Stir occasionally. Strain the
infused Cognac into a sterilised bottle,
reserving the infused dates for future use.

For the Pineapple Coconut Simple
Syrup, simply mix together the pineapple
juice and sugar until the sugar has
completely dissolved.

To make the cocktail, combine all the
ingredients in a cocktail shaker filled
with ice and shake. Double strain into
a Turkish teacup and top with grated
coconut to garnish.

Thrills can come cheaply in Istanbul,
absorbing street life from a Beyoğlu terrace,
say, over meze platters and cloudy, liquorice-
scented glasses of raki. Those with more
prodigal preferences will assuredly be
sated at Çırağan Palace Kempinski, where
Ottoman sultans lived and frolicked in the
17th century. Attractively positioned on the
banks of the Bosphorous, it has the tranquil
manner of a resort. In the mornings, guests
preface their Topkapı Palace jaunts with
balcony breakfasts; when they return it is
time for sunbed cat naps, sudsy hammam
sessions and dips in the infinity pool. By
evening they are ready to retreat to the palm
tree garden and Le Fumoir, the bar kitted out
with lanterns and a billowing fabric ceiling.
Single malts and cigars will suffice for most,
but those with the deepest of pockets might
be curious enough to splurge on the $2,500
nightcap-ready 'Gilded Sultan's Elixir': a base
of rare Hennessy Richard Cognac married with
coconut-infused pineapple juice, honey syrup
and fig bitters, suitably garnished with a rim
of edible gold dust. Compared to checking
into the commodious Sultan Suite, prized by
royalty, it's a regal bargain.

The Gilded Sultan's Elixir isn't a cocktail
made for everyday sipping, so New York
bartender and educator Franky Marshall
made the riff (known as the Sultan's Pick-Me-
Up) reinterpreting the extravagent beverage's
ingredients through a far more accessible
lens. Enjoyed as either a nightcap or morning
reviver, it balances out the sharp fruitiness
of the pineapple with layers of bittersweet
chocolate, coffee (a nod to Turkey's richly
caffeinated history), coconut and a 'fruit and
nut' mix with dates that mellow out the Cognac
and add silkiness to the mouth feel.

No. 29

Gilded Sultan's Elixir Riff

LE FUMOIR AT THE ÇIRAĞAN PALACE KEMPINSKI, ISTANBUL, TURKEY

Created by Franky Marshall

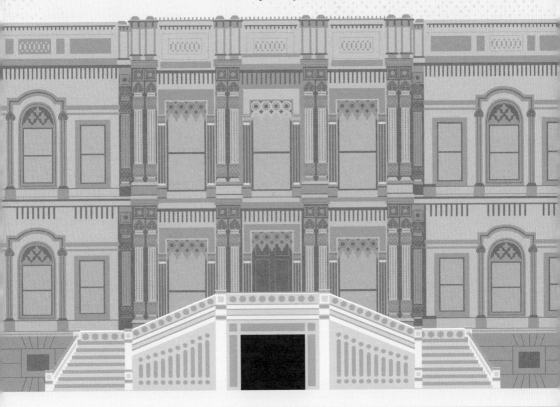

BEHIND THE BAR

No. 30

Whiskey-A-Go-Go

LIBRARY BAR
AT THE NORMAN
TEL AVIV, ISRAEL

INGREDIENTS

30 ml (1 fl oz) Spiced Pomegranate Juice*
50 ml (1¾ fl oz) rye whiskey
20 ml (⅔ fl oz) lemongrass syrup
20 ml (⅔ fl oz) freshly squeezed lemon juice
1 star anise, to garnish

*For the Spiced Pomegranate Juice
(makes 1 litre/34 fl oz):
1 litre (34 fl oz) pomegranate juice
6 cloves
6 cardamom pods, crushed
8–10 pink peppercorns

METHOD

For the Spiced Pomegranate Juice, combine all the ingredients in a non-reactive container and refrigerate overnight. Strain in a sterilised container and store for up to 72 hours in the refrigerator.

To make the cocktail, combine the ingredients in a cocktail shaker filled with ice and shake well. Double strain into a Martini glass and garnish with a star anise.

White City, Tel Aviv's residential enclave of Bauhaus-style buildings, received a dose of modernity when The Norman (named for Norman Lourie, the South African-born filmmaker and founder of Israel's first luxury resort, Dolphin House) opened across two circa-1920s buildings in 2014. When they aren't at the rooftop infinity pool ogling the Mediterranean Sea, or in their suites with the brilliant ceramic tiles, French doors and writing desks, there's a good chance that guests are in the bar. True to its name, Library Bar provides them with an assortment of books to pore over should they feel so inclined. Some do, others can't keep their eyes off this joint, which whispers of the 1940s with a burnished pewter bar, hexagonal stools and bouquets poking out of vases. Classics, including the underrated 'Bamboo' and 'Angel's Share', are on the cocktail menu, but better to sample the region's culinary bounty with signature drinks that make way for the likes of Jaffa oranges. Norman gin, made in collaboration with the Israeli Jullius Distillery, combining dates, almonds, citrons and Galilee herbs, is the spirited backbone of the 'First Date', with lemon juice, date syrup and grapefruit just picked from the hotel's garden.

Pomegranate juice spiffs up the Whiskey-A-Go-Go and gives it Israeli flair. Although the Library Bar creates a sous-vide blend of freshly squeezed pomegranate, cardamom, pink peppercorns and cloves, home bartenders can follow the easier variation here.

No. 31

Burj Royale

SKYVIEW BAR &
RESTAURANT AT
BURJ AL ARAB JUMEIRAH,
DUBAI, UAE

INGREDIENTS

20 ml (⅔ fl oz) Grey Goose
   La Vanille vanilla vodka
10 ml (⅓ fl oz) Chambord
10 ml (⅓ fl oz) Monin gum syrup
1–2 fresh raspberries
1–2 fresh blackberries
100 ml (3½ fl oz) Louis Roederer
   Brut Premier Champagne
edible gold dust, to garnish

METHOD

Muddle all the ingredients except
the Champagne in a cocktail
shaker, then shake. Double strain
into a chilled Martini glass, then
pour the Champagne over a bar
spoon to layer on top. Garnish
with edible gold dust.

Futuristic high-rises dominate Dubai's
ever-changing skyline, yet Burj Al Arab,
the seemingly fluttering sail-shaped hotel
designed by British architect Tom Wright,
is undoubtedly one of the most wondrous
and enduring. When it opened in 1999, the
all-suite Burj Al Arab was a turning point for
Dubai, shaping the emirate's narrative of a
desert-turned-megalopolis ruled by illusion.
Ascending from a man-made island, the steel-
glass-aluminium skyscraper with the towering
atrium and bevy of butlers encapsulates over-
the-top grandeur; a place where choosing
from nearly 20 different types of pillows to
sleep on, running your hand over 24-carat gold
leaf, and splashing around in pools prettified
with 10 million mosaic tiles is the norm.

Shisha smoking unfolds in the aptly shiny
Gold on 27, complemented by cocktails such
as 'Scent of the Souk', with apricot- and
fig-infused gin, baharat-spiced syrup and
mastika. On the same floor, ask for a Vesper or
a non-boozy smoked-honey Old Fashioned with
King Pu-Erh and barrel-aged oolong teas at
Skyview Bar & Restaurant. Arabian Gulf vistas
are magnified through the glass walls and the
ceiling, plastered with blue and green lights,
is sheer Dubai flamboyance.

THE MIDDLE EAST/AFRICA/SOUTH ASIA/ASIA

A ROOM
WITH
A VIEW

Imbibing while taking in an eye-popping vista is a particularly intoxicating combination. Try it at one of these hotels.

LUX Belle Mare Resort & Villas, Mauritius: At this Kelly Hoppen-designed boutique resort on the beach, nestled inside tropical gardens close to the village of Belle Mare, sounds of the Indian Ocean will tease you out of bed for a Mauritian kheer breakfast. Much later, say goodbye to the day at Mari Kontan, the darling cabana-style poolside hut that narrates the island's history, with over 100 different types of rum to taste.

Six Senses Laamu, Maldives: Guests trek to remote Laamu Atoll to stay in one of the beachfront or over-water thatched villas at Six Senses Laamu. When they are done with their slate of open-air yoga classes and Ayurvedic treatments, they scatter off to the over-water Chill Bar and wait for the DJ with an 'Abandon Ship' (Corralejo Blanco tequila, mango-coriander [cilantro] cordial, pineapple, citrus and spicy fire-water tincture), or plop down onto one of the low-slung wooden stools at Sip Sip, the sunken bar that looks onto the Indian Ocean, with a 'Maldivian Milk Punch' (Bacardi rum, aged arrack and spiced syrup).

AYANA Resort and Spa, Bali: On a cliff-top above Jimbaran Bay, AYANA has a dozen swimming pools and butler-serviced villas tucked into the gardens. Rock Bar is maybe the most striking aspect of the property, despite the uncomfortable crowds who also want to see the sun slink into the horizon, 14 metres (46 feet) above the Indian Ocean, with a chamomile-infused gin and tonic or a kaffir-leaf 'Lychee Martini'.

Halekulani, Hawaii: Halekulani first started welcoming weary fishermen on Honolulu's Waikiki Beach in 1883; by 1907, it was a full-fledged hotel. A hit with honeymooners, Halekulani promises strawberry-basil Martinis and live jazz at the living room-like Lewers Lounge, but the real treat is the indoor-outdoor House Without a Key. Sitting underneath the more-than-a-century-old kiawe tree, looking onto Diamond Head and serenaded by the quirky ukulele, is the ideal way to become acquainted with their signature Mai Tai.

Hotel Il Pellicano, Porto Ercole, Italy: Italy comes alive – and teems with tourists – in the summertime. Pay no mind to the hordes at Il Pellicano, a countryside hide-out on the Tuscan coast between Rome and Pisa (in 1965 a couple stole away here for secretive trysts before it became a hotel). Leave your own bougainvillea-drenched terrace for the one at Bar All'Aperto, where the sea views are accompanied by a Martini tinged with Campania-made mandarinetto liqueur.

Hotel du Cap–Eden-Roc, Antibes, France: A French Riviera legend since its inception as a villa for intellectuals in 1870, Hotel du Cap–Eden-Rock has seen its fair share of royalty and celebrities, including the Duke and Duchess of Windsor, Rita Hayworth and Pablo Picasso. With an infinity pool carved into the rocks and secluded cabanas, it continues to provide recreational bliss to the posh guests. One of their favourite spots to feast on the Mediterranean Sea is on the curving terrace of Eden-Roc Bar, a 'Fancy Fizz' (Bombay Sapphire gin, ginger beer, lemon juice, agave syrup and lemongrass) by their side.

No. 32

Not For Everybody

LE CHURCHILL
AT LA MAMOUNIA,
MARRAKECH, MOROCCO

INGREDIENTS

50 ml (1¾ fl oz) Basil-Infused Gin*
20 ml (⅔ fl oz) Strawberry Shrub**
**50 ml (1¾ fl oz) freshly pressed
strawberry juice**
3 drops of rosemary bitters
fresh rosemary sprig, to garnish

*** For the Basil-Infused Gin
(makes 700 ml/24 fl oz):**
700 ml (24 fl oz) Beefeater 24 gin
50 g (2 oz) fresh basil leaves

***** For the Strawberry Shrub
(makes 1 litre/34 fl oz):**
**1 kg (2 lb 4 oz) fresh strawberries,
hulled and quartered**
1 kg (2 lb 4 oz) Demerara sugar
500 ml (17 fl oz) red wine vinegar

METHOD

For the Basil-Infused Gin, combine the gin and basil in a non-reactive container, then store in a dry, dark place for 14 days. Strain the gin into a sterilised, airtight container and refrigerate for up to 2 months.

For the Strawberry Shrub, combine the strawberries and sugar in a container, cover and refrigerate for 72 hours. Combine the mixture in a saucepan and cook on a low temperature until it has reduced by a fifth. Let cool, then add the vinegar. Strain it into a sterilised container and refrigerate for up to 2 months.

To make the cocktail, combine all the ingredients in a cocktail shaker filled with ice. Strain into glass filled with ice and garnish with a rosemary sprig.

The Man Who Knew Too Much, the 1956 Alfred Hitchcock thriller starring a 'Que Sera, Sera'-singing Doris Day, centres on a family unwittingly swept up in an assassination plot while on holiday in Morocco. Fans of La Mamounia will instantly recognise the majestic hotel's light red ochre façade on screen, for it is as deeply entrenched in Marrakech culture as the nearby medina's dusty streets. La Mamounia, a medley of traditional Moroccan architecture and Art-Deco pizzazz, opened in 1923, on the 18th-century grounds that Sultan Sidi Mohammed ben Abdallah gifted to his son Mamoun. It was adored by the celebrity set, but the guest who might have loved the La Mamounia best was Winston Churchill. He first fell for La Mamounia and Marrakech, the city he dubbed the 'Paris of the Sahara', on a painting holiday in the 1930s. Every winter he kept returning. Much of La Mamounia has changed since the statesman marvelled at the shifting light of the Atlas Mountains, but not those expansive gardens with the striking slew of olive trees and rose bushes. Wander through them, and then sit in dark, jazzy Le Churchill for another fleeting nip of days gone by.

No. 33

Sarova Stanley Spinner

EXCHANGE BAR AT
SAROVA STANLEY,
NAIROBI, KENYA

INGREDIENTS

30 ml (1 fl oz) Martini extra dry
  vermouth
30 ml (1 fl oz) Campari
30 ml (1 fl oz) gin
30 ml (1 fl oz) Cointreau
pared orange zest, to garnish

METHOD

Combine all the ingredients
in a cocktail shaker filled with
ice and shake. Strain into a Martini
glass over a large ice cube and
garnish with the orange zest.

Nairobi's evolution from ramshackle swamp territory to African metropolis was propelled by construction of the railway, kicking off in 1896 in the then Kenyan capital of Mombasa. By 1902, Nairobi had gradually developed and so Mayence Bent began operating a boarding house for railway employees, feeding guests with produce from her husband's farm. When the Great Fire of Victoria Street destroyed the building, the undeterred Bent moved to a new location and opened the two-story Stanley, the city's first hotel, where one could ooh and ahh at Mount Kilimanjaro from the veranda. Now part of Kenya's Sarova Hotels & Resorts, the Stanley does an impressive job of remembering the past – one marked by visits from Frank Sinatra, then-Princess Elizabeth and Ernest Hemingway – by keeping such elements as the black-and-white floor in the lobby up to snuff. Awash with red leather and mahogany, the Exchange Bar, then called Long Bar, is the former headquarters of Nairobi's first stock exchange, founded in 1954. Under the woven palm fans suspended from the ceiling, now it's loads of business travellers who converse over rum coladas and banana daiquiris.

The traditional three-equal-parts approach to a Negroni is vivified by the presence of Cointreau in this cocktail, leading to flavours reminiscent of an Aperol Spritz – sans the bubbles.

SPOTLIGHT:
SAFARI
for the love of nature's happy hour

WHERE THE WILD THINGS ARE

At Royal Chundu Island Lodge, in Katambora, Zambia, guests spend their days on a boat safari, floating across the Zambezi River and scoping out elephants, hippos, waterbuck and crocodiles. They also make time for excursions to Victoria Falls, walk through baobab trees, go tiger fishing, and wake up early for sunrise cruises. When those activities all come to a rest, when darkness will soon shroud the sky, folks will gather at the River Lodge before dinner takes place around the fire for one last burst of saturated colour. Most of them will be holding a gin and tonic.

African sunsets are a sight to behold every evening, tinting the sky in a collision of deep red and orange hues. The ritual of the sundowner, sipping while marvelling at the sun dipping and vanishing, can be traced back to 19th-century Africa, when British officers, exhausted from a long day in the bush, would revive with a cooling, dusk-time nip of gin. Since those colonial days, the quenching pastime has evolved. The drink is largely a gin and tonic now, and it's an essential component of any African holiday, particularly contemplative safaris.

Safari accommodations are not like typical hotels, and their bars are small and well-edited; these are not the places to try new-fangled mezcal drinks with homemade tinctures. Most drinks served here are straightforward and satisfying, woven into all-inclusive packages. Some of them, like the camps and lodges operated by the sustainable-minded Singita in South Africa, Tanzania, Zimbabwe and Rwanda, have field guides who are ready to ply guests with gin and tonics from the fully stashed cooler boxes on their vehicles. In Africa, there isn't a dramatic interior to look forward to come happy hour, but the landscape. Even the most brilliant of designers cannot compete with quaffing a cocktail as a giraffe streaks by.

Guests at Singita Kwitonda Lodge, at the edge of Volcanoes National Park in Rwanda, can unwind with a chilled whisky in their private heated plunge pool after a dusty gorilla trek, just as at Royal Malewane, in South Africa's Greater Kruger National Park, tented, lantern-lit bush dinners are preceded by an alfresco sampling of the hotel's massive whisky collection.

The sundowner, then, is a colossal yet simple reminder that travelling is an unparallelled opportunity to celebrate, and deepen a connection with, Mother Nature.

No. 34

Passion Fruit Gin Cocktail

THE TRAVELLERS BAR
AT THE ROYAL LIVINGSTONE
VICTORIA FALLS ZAMBIA
HOTEL BY ANANTARA,
LIVINGSTONE, ZAMBIA

INGREDIENTS

50 ml (1¾ fl oz) dry gin (the bar
uses Mundambi, specially made
for the hotel by South Africa's
New Harbour Distillery)
25 ml (¾ fl oz) triple sec
2¼ teaspoons freshly squeezed
lemon juice
5 ml (1 teaspoon) passion fruit
purée
2 drops of Angostura bitters
pared lemon zest, to garnish

METHOD

Combine all the ingredients except
the bitters in a cocktail shaker
filled with ice and shake well.
Strain into a rocks glass filled with
ice, then add the Angostura bitters
and garnish with lemon zest.

In the mid-19th century, David Livingstone, the Scottish physician, missionary and explorer of southern and central Africa, was apparently the first European to come across a waterfall on the Zambezi River, at the border of Zambia and Zimbabwe. It was called Mosi-oa-Tunya ('The Smoke That Thunders') in the local Lozi language, but Livingstone, ever the loyal Brit, decided to name it for Queen Victoria. Considered the largest waterfall in the world, Victoria Falls is certainly a marvellous sight. Imagine, then, waking up to a whirring ceiling fan in your creamy, Colonial-style suite, breakfasting on the veranda, and then trotting over to this cascading spectacle in just five minutes. At the resort, located within Mosi-oa-Tunya National Park, it always appears as if you are on safari. Wildlife freely roams the grounds, so it's perfectly plausible that you'll be gobsmacked by a moseying zebra as you finish the remains of a cappuccino. Before a dinner aboard the old-timey locomotive that chugs its way through the Zambezi River Valley, partake of a gin sundowner in The Travellers Bar. Throbbing with guests on stitched leather chairs, it has live piano music that will woo you into returning for a cheeky bedtime send-off.

No. 35

Rose Ginvino

THE WILLASTON BAR
AT THE SILO HOTEL,
CAPE TOWN,
SOUTH AFRICA

INGREDIENTS

50 ml (1¾ fl oz) South African
    Musgrave rose gin
25 ml (¾ fl oz) Marras
    chenin blanc
25 ml (¾ fl oz) freshly squeezed
    lime juice
25 ml (¾ fl oz) freshly squeezed
    grapefruit juice
20 ml (⅔ fl oz) rose syrup
1 egg white
rose petals, to garnish

METHOD

Combine all the ingredients in
a cocktail shaker, adding the egg
white last, then top up with ice and
shake well. Strain into a Martini
glass and garnish with rose petals.

Powerfully intertwining the past and present
on Cape Town's V&A Waterfront is Zeitz
MOCAA. A trove of contemporary art from
Africa and its diaspora, it was fashioned out
of a derelict 1924 grain-silo complex by
London's Heatherwick Studio, and was the
tallest building in sub-Saharan Africa at
one point. Directly above the museum, in
the former elevator tower, is The Silo Hotel.
Opened in 2017, featuring a private art
gallery and panoramic rooftop pool, it is
a commanding presence, with 'pillow'
windows that soften the well-preserved
concrete exterior. Inside, the industrial
tone gives way to exuberance, the crystal
chandelier-speckled guest rooms a profusion
of colour – behold the baths with a view and
those glimmering black-and-white striped
floors. Named for the first ship to export grain
to Europe, the sixth-floor Willaston Bar is
just as vivid. Park yourself on a teal bar stool
or one of the deep blue-green semi-circular
banquettes and request an 'Iceplant Negroni'
with Turkish fig-infused Bombay Sapphire gin
and Aperol. Through those bubbles of bloated
glass, you'll be nothing short of transfixed
by the appearance of Table Mountain and
the harbour.

THE SILO HOTEL
CAPE TOWN, SOUTH AFRICA

No. 36

Aberfeldy
Fashion

THE CLUB BAR
AND CIGAR LOUNGE
AT THE OBEROI,
NEW DELHI, INDIA

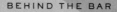

INGREDIENTS

50 ml (1¾ fl oz) Aberfeldy 28-Year-Old
   Single Malt Scotch
1 teaspoon maple syrup
2 dashes of Homemade Bitters*
   or Angostura orange bitters

*For the Homemade Bitters
   (makes 250 ml/8½ fl oz):
5 g (6–7) star anise
5 g (1 tablespoon) cloves
5 g (2½ teaspoons) fennel seeds
5 g (2 teaspoons) cracked Szechuan
   peppercorns
3 x 2⅓ in (10 g/½ oz) Ceylon cinnamon
   sticks
250 ml (8½ fl oz) vodka

METHOD

For the Homemade Bitters, put all
the spices in a jar and add the vodka.
Let sit in a dark place for 3 hours,
stirring the mixture every hour. Strain
into a sterilised jar or bottle. The bitters
will keep for years.

   To make the cocktail, combine all the
ingredients in a mixing glass and stir
well. Serve in an old fashioned glass
over a sphere of ice.

A less resilient entrepreneur might have
thrown in the towel if the opening of his hotel
coincided with the Indo-Pakistani War of 1965,
but M.S. Oberoi, who acquired the Grand Hotel
in Calcutta just before World War II broke out,
persevered yet again in the face of tumult.
Good thing, too, because The Oberoi, New
Delhi – the flagship of the Indian luxury hotel
brand he launched in 1934 – was the country's
first large, modern, service-oriented property,
even hiring, in an unprecedented move, female
housekeeping staff. When designer Adam D.
Tihany overhauled the hotel in 2018, a property
where Omar Sharif, Mick Jagger and countless
Bollywood stars all passed through, he was
careful to respect that heritage. It looks
lighter and fresher, but most importantly the
jali screen in the lobby that guides people
through the window-lined marble corridor,
and the furnishings that summon English
architect Edwin Lutyens, who masterminded
the design of numerous New Delhi landmarks,
are all tasteful updates. The Club Bar and
Cigar Lounge, where you'll overhear orders for
a Negroni or Cognac Alexander, is a library-like
room tinted in red and maroon. With punches
of brass and hand-knotted rugs underfoot,
it's evident that a new chapter has begun.

   To make the most out of the Aberfeldy
Fashion, do as the patrons of the Club Bar
and Cigar Lounge do and sip this one leisurely
between puffs of a woody, spice-tinged
Cohiba Robusto.

INGREDIENTS

1 teaspoon patchouli oil
45 ml (1½ fl oz) gin
30 ml (1 fl oz) fresh beetroot
   (beet) juice
25 ml (¾ fl oz) lemon and yuzu
   juice (the bar uses fresh yuzu,
   but lime is a good substitute)
15 ml (½ fl oz) Ginger Syrup*
1 fresh oyster, to serve

*For the Ginger Syrup
   (makes 500 ml/17 fl oz):
500 ml (17 fl oz) freshly pressed
   ginger juice
500 g (1 lb 2 oz) caster (superfine)
   sugar

METHOD

For the Ginger Syrup, combine
the ginger juice and sugar in a
container and let sit for 6 hours.
Fine strain. The syrup will keep in
the refrigerator for up to 3 months.
   Shake the patchouli oil with ice
for about 10 seconds, then fine
strain into a glass. Combine all
the remaining liquids in a cocktail
shaker filled with ice and shake.
Double strain the into an old
fashioned glass. Serve with
a fresh oyster on the side.

The music- and fashion-forward W Hotels
brand took a serene turn when W Maldives
opened on the private island of Fesdu in North
Ari Atoll in 2006. Reached via speedboat, the
resort is defined by a network of wooden jettys
leading to thatched-roof villas with plunge
pools, most of them poised over water with
circular windows that look onto lagoon fauna.
The aqueous landscape, stitched together
with white-sand beaches, turquoise lagoons
and reefs, means that days are peppered
with snorkelling, as well as diving and fishing
adventures. Unwinding between activities
is also a priority here – a task that's easy
to accomplish given the bungalows' swings,
circular daybeds and sun-deck loungers. Even
baths are taken enveloped in fresh air. At dusk,
curled up on an alfresco couch with a lychee
cocktail, it's the bar SIP that ensures this state
of relaxation continues. In keeping with the W
Hotels' this-could-be-a-nightclub mentality,
you'll find an energising DJ on hand, but the
main attraction is seeing the sun set in a blaze
of colour over the Indian Ocean, a poignant
pause before a barbecue repast around the
fire pit.

My Heart Beets For You

SIP AT
W MALDIVES, FESDU ISLAND,
MALDIVES

EAST ASIA
& THE PACIFIC

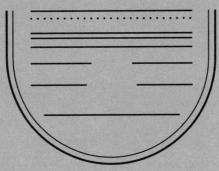

EAST ASIA & THE PACIFIC

Mayhem is rampant in Asia, yet there is a certain poetry to all those whizzing motorbikes and tuk-tuks manoeuvring their way through the automobiles inevitably at a standstill. The energy here is, at turns, bewildering, daunting and elating, and a hotel bar is a reassuring asylum after a day on the chaotic streets. Rooftop lairs, particularly popular in Australia and Bangkok, where places such as The Speakeasy at Hotel Muse are as essential to travel itineraries as a Wat Pho temple tour, have the secondary advantage of bird's-eye views over the city below. Cocktail menus in this corner of the world might increasingly mirror those glittering high-rises puncturing the crowded skylines with their out-there drinks, but there is a certain timeless civility that courses through Asian hotel bars. Captain's Bar opened at the Mandarin Oriental, Hong Kong, in 1963, and checkered glass partitions still delineate its booths, just as countless silver tankards of beer are still placed before wide-eyed guests. It is proof that tradition can peacefully co-exist with modernity.

No. 38

Lost in Translation (L.I.T.)

NEW YORK BAR
AT PARK HYATT
TOKYO, JAPAN

INGREDIENTS

40 ml (1¼ fl oz) Japanese sake
10 ml (⅓ fl oz) peach liqueur
10 ml (⅓ fl oz) Sakura liqueur
20 ml (⅔ fl oz) cranberry juice
10 ml (⅓ fl oz) freshly squeezed
  lime juice

METHOD

Combine all the ingredients in a
cocktail shaker filled with ice and
shake. Strain into a Martini glass.

Park Hyatt Tokyo might forever be enmeshed with Sofia Coppola's Academy-Award-winning 2003 film, *Lost In Translation*. Even if Bill Murray's Bob and Scarlett Johansson's Charlotte hadn't befriended each other here, high above neon-hued Shinjuku, the hotel would still exhilarate.

Encompassing the upper portion of a three-block skyscraper – one of the city's tallest – Park Hyatt Tokyo opened in 1994, designed by the late Kenzō Tange. Clean, calming lines abound in the guest rooms and a snow-capped Mount Fuji in the distance is companion to swims in one of the world's most good-looking pools.

At the very top of the hotel, on the 52nd floor, is the New York Bar (yes, this is where Bob and Charlotte first broke the ice with, 'For relaxing times, make it Suntory time'). Views of the wild, chaotic Tokyo skyline from the floor-to-ceiling windows are, of course, excellent, but they are compounded by Valerio Adami's quartet of Pop Art paintings and Japanese sirloin steaks sizzling on the grill. Like the 'Matured-Fashioned' with Woodford Reserve bourbon aged in-house, fine-grained Japanese wasanbon sugar, bitters and orange peel, New York Bar exemplifies the importance of, albeit costly, simplicity.

EAST ASIA & THE PACIFIC

IMPERIAL HOTEL,
TOKYO, JAPAN

BEHIND THE BAR

No. 39

Mount Fuji Riff

OLD IMPERIAL BAR
AT IMPERIAL HOTEL,
TOKYO, JAPAN

Created by Julia Momose

INGREDIENTS

45 ml (1½ fl oz) Suntory Roku gin
15 ml (½ oz) freshly squeezed
  lemon juice
15 ml (½ oz) simple syrup
  (page 11)
25 ml (¾ fl oz) fresh pineapple juice
25 ml (¾ fl oz) double (heavy) cream
1 egg white
1 Amarena cherry, to garnish

METHOD

Combine the ingredients in a cocktail
shaker filled with ice and shake,
then strain back into the shaker
and dry shake without ice until there
are no more ice shards. Pour into
a chilled coupe glass and garnish
with an Amarena cherry on the side
of the glass.

Close to Tokyo's Imperial Palace, Frank
Lloyd Wright, that leading light of American
architecture, completed the second
incarnation of the Imperial Hotel in 1923
(the original debuted in 1890). Designed to
capture the attention of Western tourists,
the courtyard-strewn complex was built
on a floating foundation in a gripping Mayan
Revival-meets futurist industrial style that,
despite surviving the Great Kantō Earthquake,
was heartbreakingly demolished in 1968.
Preservationists were keen to see the lobby
and reflecting pool reassembled at the
Meiji-Mura open-air architectural museum
in Inuyama. Likewise, when a new Imperial
Hotel sprouted on the former site in 1970,
they rejoiced that the Old Imperial Bar's
design made way for terracotta and Oyā
stone salvaged from the Wright era. Aside
from these gorgeous remnants of the 1920s,
it is a deliciously old-school establishment,
suggesting a time when A-listers such as
Charlie Chaplin, Marilyn Monroe and Joe
DiMaggio hid away at the hotel. Sit at the bar,
its counter glowing with a symmetrical row
of warm spotlights, and let the courteous
bartenders make Martinis, pour Scotch over
flawless cubes of ice, and replenish your
kaki-pi, the addictive rice cracker and peanut
bar snack that supposedly originated here.

It's been served at the Old Imperial Bar
for decades and still the exact recipe for the
Mount Fuji, named for the volcano that Frank
Lloyd Wright so adored, remains a mystery.
Incorporating the six ingredients that star
in the Mount Fuji, Julia Momose, creative
director at the Japanese-inspired Chicago bar
Kumiko, made her own rendition of the drink.

IT HAPPENED ONE DAY

When Caravelle Saigon opened, in 1959, it was considered one of Vietnam's tallest and most modern buildings, but this welcome dose of luxury couldn't alleviate the grief and unpredictability that hung in the air in the wake of the still-raging Vietnam War that had started in 1955. Five years later, for instance, a bomb would explode on the Caravelle's fifth floor. If there was a comforting element to this new hotel, it was the presence of the Saigon Saigon Rooftop Bar because here politicians, international journalists such as Peter Jennings (the Saigon bureaus of ABC, CBS and NBC set up shop at the Caravelle in the 1960s) and soldiers alike could congregate over beers and watch the war underway on the other side of the Saigon River from its balconies and terraces.

Less intense are the tales of these American hotels steeped in political and cultural history:

The Hay-Adams, Washington, DC: This hotel is a tribute to bigwigs John Hay (the former Secretary of State and personal secretary to Abraham Lincoln) and William Adams (a historian, Harvard professor and scion of the presidential Adams family). A short walk to the White House, which opened in 1928, on the site where Hay and Adams once held lively salons in their Romanesque homes that attracted the likes of Mark Twain and Henry James. Off the Record seems like an old bar, but it isn't (it arrived in 1980s). Still, the caricatures of political movers and shakers on the walls, and the Pear Martini-stoked happy hours on the red-tufted sofas hark back to a time when politicians, all the more zealous after a few rounds of Old Fashioneds, swapped secrets and plotted strategies.

The Roosevelt New Orleans: Seymour Weiss, owner of the Roosevelt New Orleans hotel, now part of the Waldorf Astoria collection, was buddies with Louisiana Governor and United States Senator Huey P. Long, who maintained a suite on the 12th floor of the hotel. The politician's favourite drink was the frothy, labour-intensive 'Ramos Gin Fizz'. He loved it so much that in 1935, as a publicity stunt, he finagled the Roosevelt's then head bartender Sam Guarino to come up to New York and show the misguided staff at the New Yorker Hotel how to confidently make the drink. Named for the official cocktail of New Orleans, the Sazerac Bar debuted at the Roosevelt in 1949 and on opening day, a band of ladies – in the old incarnation of the bar women were only allowed to attend during Mardi Gras – showed up for what has been heralded as the Stormin' of the Sazerac. Today, the Paul Ninas Art Deco murals and African wood panelling are suggestive of that mid-century promise, especially since many of those guests seated in club chairs will be waiting on a Ramos Gin Fizz.

The Algonquin Hotel Times Square, New York: Two-dollar-a-night beds was the going rate when the Algonquin Hotel Times Square opened in 1902. Purported to be the oldest and longest continuously operating hotel in New York, it is most fêted for the daily, booze-soaked Round Table lunches that transpired here for more than a decade among writers such as Dorothy Parker, Alexander Woollcott, Robert Benchley and *The New Yorker* founder Harold Ross. By 1923, the first of the Algonquin's resident felines became another off-the-wall fixture of the hotel. That optimistic, post-World-War-I literary spirit has surely faded, but if you use your imagination, The Blue Bar, which opened right after the end of Prohibition, can still whisk you away to another decade with its strong Rob Roy cocktail and fusillade of blue light.

Hotel Jerome, Aspen, Colorado: In the late 19th century, the Colorado Silver Boom put Aspen on the map, and ever since Macy's department store president, Jerome Wheeler, opened it in 1889, Hotel Jerome has played a part in the city's ascent from mining town to chi-chi ski resort. After the crash in 1893, Hotel Jerome managed to stay afloat as a boarding house, but after World War II celebrities started coming to stay at the renovated hotel on their ski sojourns. In 1970, when Hunter S. Thompson bizarrely ran for Pitkin County sheriff, he made the Jerome's J-Bar his de facto office. A little wild-west kitschy, the rustic bar is where to go for subdued aprés-ski revelry and the 'Aspen Crud', a vanilla-ice-cream milkshake spiked with shots of Jim Beam bourbon that was invented at the J-Bar when it was forced to transition into a G-rated soda fountain during Prohibition.

Hark back to a time
when politicians,
all the more zealous
after a few rounds
of Old Fashioneds,
swapped secrets and
plotted strategies.

INGREDIENTS

45 ml (1½ fl oz) London Dry Gin
15 ml (½ fl oz) Bokbunja raspberry wine
10 ml (⅓ fl oz) Fino sherry
5 ml (1 teaspoon) crème de cassis
3 dashes of Peychaud's bitters
3 dashes of absinthe
15 ml (½ fl oz) Honey Water*
15 ml (½ fl oz) freshly squeezed
   lemon juice
½ teaspoon egg white

*For the Honey Water
   (makes 120 ml/4 fl oz):
90 ml (3 fl oz) honey
30 ml (1 fl oz) hot water

METHOD

For the Honey Water, combine the
honey and hot water in a jar and stir.
Refrigerate until chilled.
   To make the cocktail, combine all the
ingredients in a cocktail shaker and dry
shake with no ice until foamy, then add
ice to the shaker and shake again.
Double strain into a Nick & Nora glass.

Decades before bars – and bartenders –
acquired a celebrity sheen, there was the
bon vivant Charles H. Baker Jr. A New York
magazine writer, he inherited a sizable
chunk of cash that funded a life-changing
round-the-world cruise. His chronicles
of mysterious cocktails sipped in far-
flung locales led to the publication of *The
Gentleman's Companion* in 1939. Baker, whose
droll book of anecdotes and recipes is prized in
bartending circles, would surely have felt right
at home in this swish bar named for him.
   Opened in 2015, its design scheme merges
two disparate sources of inspiration – New
England speakeasies and Korean royal palace
dress and ornamentation – translating to
stand-outs such as metal panelling cast
on stingray skins and a glass mosaic that
suggests the technique of mother-of-pearl
inlaid on lacquerware.
   Cocktail menus change here, and so one
themed around Baker's travels to Mexico, say,
would yield herbal creations like the crystalline
'Ms Frida' with tequila, grapefruit, lavender
cordial, bergamot and tonic. 'Remember the
Maine', the cocktail of rye, sweet vermouth,
Cherry Heering and absinthe, which Baker
discovered in Havana during the 1933 Sergeants'
Revolt and later immortalised in the pages
of his book, is always a worthy order.

Raspberry Calling

CHARLES H.
AT THE FOUR SEASONS HOTEL,
SEOUL, SOUTH KOREA

Created by Keith Motsi

EAST ASIA & THE PACIFIC

BEHIND THE BAR

No. 41

Moods of Love

LONG BAR AT
WALDORF ASTORIA
SHANGHAI ON THE
BUND, SHANGHAI,
CHINA

INGREDIENTS

60 ml (2 fl oz) Michter's bourbon
20 ml (⅔ fl oz) peach liqueur
10 ml (⅓ fl oz) freshly squeezed
  lemon juice
10 ml (⅓ fl oz) Luxardo triple sec

METHOD

Combine the ingredients in a cocktail
shaker filled with ice and shake.
Double strain into a Champagne flute.

The origins of Long Bar – which opened when Waldorf Astoria did in 2010 – are distinctly undemocratic. In 1910, when privileged members of the snooty British colonials-only Shanghai Club began roosting in the building, its bar – then the longest in the Far East – was explicitly hierarchical. Women were banned entirely from the L-shaped mahogany bar, and only those gents of a particularly exclusive breed were allowed to perch in hallowed territory over by the window; the less socially fortunate were relegated to the back.

Today's everyone-welcome version of Long Bar was faithfully recreated through archival photos, and is matched with marble tables, stained glass and live jazz.

A 'Seaman's Fizz' (Havana Club rum, rosemary-honey syrup, grapefruit juice, cream, egg white) commemorates the Shanghai Club's 1956 changeover to the Seaman's Club, but the 'Colonel Sanders Margarita', with bacon-infused tequila and homemade pineapple and lemongrass purée, pays homage to Long Bar's wackier fast-food roots: in the room where that now disassembled bar once stood, the fried chicken-scented kitchen of Shanghai's first KFC outpost debuted in 1989.

No. 42

Blue Moon

LOBSTER BAR AND GRILL
AT ISLAND SHANGRI-LA,
HONG KONG

Created by Paolo De Venuto

4

INGREDIENTS

50 ml (1¾ fl oz) Absolut vodka
25 ml (¾ fl oz) blue Curaçao
20 ml (⅔ fl oz) St-Germain liqueur
5 ml (1 teaspoon) absinthe
30 ml (1 fl oz) freshly squeezed
   lemon juice
20 ml (⅔ fl oz) egg white
15 ml (½ fl oz) Cornflake Syrup*
1 cornflake, to garnish

*For the Cornflake Syrup
   (makes 2 litres/70 fl oz):
400 g (14 oz) cornflakes
2 litres (70 fl oz) mineral water
1 kg (2 lb 4 oz) caster (superfine)
   sugar

METHOD

For the Cornflake Syrup, combine
the cornflakes and 1 litre (34 fl oz)
of mineral water and mix with
a hand-held blender. Strain the
mixture, reserving the cornflakes
and discarding the excess water.
Place the cornflake pulp into a
saucepan with the sugar over a
medium heat and stir until dissolved.
Cool the syrup and pour into a
sterilised bottle. It will keep up
to two weeks in the refrigerator.
   To make the cocktail, dry shake
all the ingredients with no ice or
mix with a hand-held blender in
a cocktail shaker for better foam.
Shake again, then strain into a
rocks glass over a single ice cube.
Garnish with a cornflake.

There is no shortage of hotspots in Hong Kong
and several of them are in hotels. Still, Lobster
Bar and Grill is packed every night. A mainstay
since opening at the Island Shangri-La, Hong
Kong, in 1991 (stop in the lobby to regard the
grandiose chandeliers), it has the attractive air
of a cosmopolitan lounge, the kind of joint that
present-day nightlife sees too little of. Well-
worn, however, doesn't mean stodgy. At least,
not here.

   One of the reasons Lobster Bar and Grill
still resonates with so many is that there are
rousing drinks on the thematic menus. On
one that calls forth the 1933 James Hilton
novel Lost Horizon, there is an Asian riff on the
Gimlet, for instance, with apple liqueur, pomelo
syrup and turmeric. An ingenious old fashioned
(Michter's bourbon, brown sugar, pink salt and
chocolate) also gets the Far East treatment
with the addition of toasted rice. Even a vodka
Martini is reimagined here, with seaweed
butter, oyster leaf and caviar stimulating lusty
marine notes. A polite, outgoing staff, happy to
engage in banter, only sweetens the evening.

   Inspired by the green-blue river that weaves
through the scenic Blue Moon Valley in Yunnan,
China, bartender Paolo De Venuto created this
drink. It's whimsically bolstered by cornflakes
– one of his favourite childhood snacks.

No. 43

Thaijito

THE BAMBOO BAR AT
MANDARIN ORIENTAL,
BANGKOK, THAILAND

INGREDIENTS

1 slice of fresh root ginger
1 slice of fresh lemongrass
3 wedges of lime
1 teaspoon brown sugar
60 ml (2 fl oz) Mekhong Thai Spirit
10 ml (⅓ fl oz) freshly squeezed
  lime juice
10 ml (⅓ fl oz) simple syrup
  (page 11)

METHOD

Muddle the ginger, lemongrass,
lime and brown sugar in the bottom
of a rocks glass. Add crushed ice,
then stir in the Mehkong, lime juice
and simple syrup.

Thailand was still known as Siam when the Oriental, now part of the Mandarin Oriental collection, opened on the Chao Phraya River in 1876. As the kingdom's first luxury hotel, it courted royalty, but a fair share of writers, such as W. Somerset Maugham, Joseph Conrad and Graham Greene, also camped out here. The Authors' Lounge, coveted daily for afternoon tea, is an airy, white-washed shrine to that literary history. Guests who yearn for cocktails, not Darjeeling tea, know that the Bamboo Bar, at the other end of the hotel, awaits. Bangkok's first jazz venue, it traces back to 1953. All these years later, it's still the turf of musicians, only now they perform in a sleek room that retains its tropical modernist character with walls of glowing bottles and tiger print juxtaposed with rattan.

The Thaijito, a twist on the Mojito made with Thailand's own Mehkong, a spirit that's not quite a whiskey, not quite a rum, is quaffed regularly here, but the bar also conceives special menus, like the Compass. By trying drinks laced with ingredients such as cashew nuts, bee pollen and coconut flower, bar-goers take a sensory tour of Thailand.

MANDARIN ORIENTAL, BANGKOK, THAILAND

EAST ASIA & THE PACIFIC

SPOTLIGHT:
MENU DESIGN
flights of fancy to whet the appetite

SUM OF ITS PARTS

A room that leaves you breathless, or at least allows you to suspend a humdrum reality over the course of a Manhattan or two, and barkeeps who whip up cocktails with surprising combinations of ingredients are the hallmarks of great hotel bars. But hotel bars, given their power to eradicate everyday routines, can – and often do – push the envelope with their intricate narratives. Some might call this method novelty, but it's merely succumbing to a personal idea of wonderland.

Entry to ROOM 309 at The Pottinger Hong Kong, for example, is invitation-only. At 'reception', a guest receives a key card that grants them access to the clandestine third-floor parlour. There, in a 22-seat den flaunting antique lion-head wood pillars, they choose from two different menus by Tasting Group's Antonio Lai. One is devoted to Golden Key Classics like the French 75; the other to 'invisible' elixirs including the 'Crystal Old Fashioned' (peanut-butter bourbon, homemade wood-chip bitters, banana concentrate), listed, of course, on a transparent menu.

At the bi-level, mid-century-styled Jigger & Pony, inside the Amara Singapore, patrons settle in for the evening with a 'Madame President' (a Negroni that telegraphs the Singapore Botanic Gardens with Monkey 47 gin, kaffir dry vermouth, orchid and bitter-melon liqueur) with a playful Campari lollipop. The carbonated Mineral Vodka Soda with lime-infused Belvedere and birch sap is another common nightcap order. Both have appeared on Jigger & Pony menus, which are always creatively laid out like a magazine.

Brandishing such catchy cover lines as 'The Decade Ahead', its pages are divvied-up among the different drinks, revealing their stories in the form of newsy articles and culminating with a grid of all the cocktails conveniently listed on the back of each 'issue'.

In Montreal, at Fairmont The Queen Elizabeth, guests at Nacarat will be handed a menu that doubles as a tasting wheel. Strewn with pictograms, it orbits through bitter, spicy, umami, sour and sweet profiles, helping stumped imbibers make informed choices when they land on cocktails like the zippy 'Toadka' (vodka, white vermouth, sweet peas, mint cream, mushroom-wasabi tincture) and bourbon-raspberry 'La Marsa', redolent of Tunisia with (bell) pepper sorbet and citrus foam.

Cocktail menus are equally imaginative at Midnight Rambler, the Dallas lair from husband-and-wife duo Christy Pope and Chad Solomon inside the Joule hotel (Pagan Ritual: Rites of Spring, or the holiday-season-ready Island of Misfit Drinks). But the list is only one piece of an evocative puzzle. There are also the neo-classical cocktails embracing modernist techniques such as the 'Savoury Hunter' (lemongrass- and makrut-leaf gin, lime, coconut, coriander [cilantro], Thai chilli) and 'Tiger Style' (Batavia arrack, calamansi, palm sugar, pippali, egg white, cassia aromatic essence); and a rock 'n' roll aura thanks to dark leather, metallic finishes and a terrazzo checkerboard floor. The playlist, including tunes from The Sonics, The Velvet Underground, Ike and Tina Turner, and The Rolling Stones, was also carefully assembled to channel the 1960s and 70s. 'Hotel bars lend themselves to fantasy and escapism,' says Pope, which, adds Solomon, 'allows for more experimentation both with the overall experience, and the drinks themselves in terms of flavours and service presentation.'

To guests, a hotel bar might have the feel of a beautifully orchestrated mirage, but behind the scenes they are propelled by efficiency and practicality. 'One of the most interesting challenges I'm regularly faced with is underbar layout, meaning the nuts and bolts of bar equipment to create working spaces for bartenders. A thoughtful bar will save thousands of dollars in labour every year, reducing the amount of time it takes to execute service,' says Mike Ryan, head of bars at Kimpton Hotels & Restaurants. 'The staff should be able to focus on serving guests, not just drinks. The constant challenge is to create spaces that are functional as well as beautiful – like a majestic, four-dimensional crossword puzzle, but with booze and glass and stainless steel instead of vowels and consonants.'

A hotel bar
might have the feel
of a beautifully
orchestrated mirage,
but behind the scenes
they are propelled
by efficiency
and practicality.

No. 44

Singapore Sling

LONG BAR AT
RAFFLES SINGAPORE

Created by Ngiam Tong Boon

INGREDIENTS

30 ml (1 fl oz) Widges London Dry Gin
10 ml (⅓ fl oz) Bénédictine
10 ml (⅓ fl oz) Pierre Ferrand
  Dry Curaçao
10 ml (⅓ fl oz) Luxardo Cherry
  Sangue Morlacco
10 ml (⅓ fl oz) Crawley's Singapore
  Sling Grenadine
60 ml (2 fl oz) fresh pineapple juice
22.5 ml (scant ¾ oz) freshly
  squeezed lime juice
a dash of Scrappy's Spice
  Plantation bitters
cherry and pineapple chunk,
  to garnish

METHOD

Combine all the ingredients in a cocktail
shaker filled with ice and shake vigorously
for about 12 seconds. Strain the cocktail
into a chilled highball glass. Garnish
with a skewer of cherry and pineapple.

Champalimaud Design's restoration of Raffles Singapore in 2019 has unleashed a spurt of renewed interest in this hotel with the ethereal ivory wedding-cake façade. Dating back to 1887, the hotel has pep once more, with buffed eucalyptus and marble floors and a floral-inspired chandelier drenched in crystals taking centre-stage in the triple-story lobby. Long Bar enthusiasts need not fret because the palm fans are still in place and the peanut shells continue to litter the floor.

What has changed, for the better, is the recipe for Long Bar's signature Singapore Sling. Over the years, the drink – invented in 1915 by bartender Ngiam Tong Boon – had, critics demurred, gone downhill; its too-sweet, too-fruity taste profile an affront to all those cocktail warriors beneficently advancing palates. Long Bar's current variation harks back to the early 20th-century days of Boon, emphasising quality ingredients for drier, balanced results. The hallmark herbal Bénédictine liqueur is still an integral component, it's just united now with all-natural pomegranate grenadine syrup, cardamom-heavy Widges London Dry Gin, Pierre Ferrand Dry Curaçao and custom 'Spice Plantation' bitters. Have one, at least, then make the 'Golden Milk Punch', a saffron-spiced almond milk, ginger and apricot liqueur concoction honouring Rudyard Kipling's 1889 visit to Raffles, your next call.

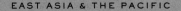
EAST ASIA & THE PACIFIC

MANHATTAN AT REGENT, SINGAPORE

No. 45

Mad Dog

MANHATTAN
AT REGENT
SINGAPORE

INGREDIENTS

60 ml (2 fl oz) Johnnie Walker
  18-year-old whisky
7.5 ml (¼ fl oz) Pierre Ferrand
  Dry Curaçao
5 ml (1 teaspoon) Luxardo
  Maraschino liqueur
5 ml (1 teaspoon) Drambuie
2 dashes of absinthe (the bar uses
  St George Absinthe Verte)
2 dashes of Angostura bitters
2 dashes of Peychaud's bitters
1 dash of Fee Brothers black
  walnut bitters
1 strip of lemon zest, to garnish

METHOD

Pour all ingredients into a mixing
glass and add ice, then stir until
chilled. Pour into a wine glass and
add a large cube of ice. Express the
lemon zest over the drink and drop
it inside the glass to garnish.

John Portman, the pioneering late American
architect and real estate developer,
invigorated hotel lobbies with futuristic
glass elevators whizzing up and down his
intricate, vertiginous atriums. When the
Pavilion InterContinental Hotel opened in
1982, it proudly ushered guests into one of
Portman's pyramid-style public spaces; today,
as Regent Singapore, that vertical design is
still an arresting focal point. Another, much
newer one, is Manhattan, the bar with 19th-
century New York undertones that opened
in 2014. Sofas for cosy tête-à-têtes and
Aviation-sipping overlap with leather, cabaret-
conjuring curtains, and the showpiece marble
bar. Manhattan has a reverence for classics,
but there is an audacious streak, too. Barrels
of ageing cocktails, for example, are stacked
in the first-ever in-hotel rickhouse. '50/50
Martinis' are plumped up with Mathilde peach
liqueur and taste-shifting garnishes of apple,
lemon peel and olive, while the 'Meyer's Fizz'
brings together Michter's US*1 Sour Mash
whiskey, vermouth, vanilla yoghurt milk punch,
clarified lemon and sparkling water. As the
'Kryptonite' (Botanist gin, Marino Secco
vermouth, clarified watermelon, mint syrup,
tonic water) and 'Bada Bing Bada Boom' (The
Glenlivet 12-Year-Old, Ruffino chianti, spice
syrup, cherry-tobacco bitters, chocolate cigar)
attest, the bar staff also have a penchant
for wit.

For dramatic flourish, Manhattan smokes
the Mad Dog with wild cherry bark and
Schisandra berries.

No. 46

Jungle Bird

AVIARY BAR AT
HILTON KUALA LUMPUR,
MALAYSIA

Adapted by Dez O'Connell

INGREDIENTS

50 ml (1¾ oz) Goslings rum
12.5 ml (2½ teaspoons) Campari
12.5 ml (2½ teaspoons) freshly
   squeezed lime juice
15 ml (½ fl oz) simple syrup (page 11)
   (1.75 parts sugar to 1 parts water)
60 ml (2 fl oz) fresh pineapple juice
1 baby pineapple, top removed
   and hollowed out, to serve
1 orange wheel, to garnish
1 pickled cherry, to garnish

METHOD

Combine all the ingredients in
a cocktail shaker filled with ice and
shake. Fill the baby pineapple vessel
with crushed ice, then strain in the
cocktail. Garnish with the orange
wheel and pickled cherry.

Had you passed through Kuala Lumpur in
the 1970s, you could have sipped a Martini
at the bar of the Hilton and watched birds
flutter through a glass wall. That phenomenon,
as rumour has it, is what spurred beverage
manager Jeffrey Ong to create the Jungle
Bird in 1973, a welcome drink coinciding with
the opening of the hotel. Served in a showy
ceramic bird vessel, it was a refreshing mix of
rum, Campari, lime juice and sugar, garnished
with fruit and flowers, that soon found its way
into the tiki canon — less sweet (thanks to
bitter Campari) and less complicated than
its brethren.

The Hilton, which attracted guests such as
Muhammad Ali and then-Princess Elizabeth
through the years, turned into a Crowne Plaza
and was eventually demolished. However,
there's a new Hilton Kuala Lumpur in the city,
and its bar is called Aviary. There are no birds
on display, but this time around there is no
need for the cruel carnival side show. In Aviary,
next to the sexy curved wall, a good ol' Jungle
Bird provides the night's requisite dose of fun.

This tiki classic is best drunk out of a
colourful, retro-style bird-shaped vessel.
Since there's a dearth of those up for grabs
at flea markets, an in-vogue baby pineapple
also provides the requisite dose of Polynesian
kitsch for this adaptation from Budapest-
based Dez O'Connell, who oversees cocktails
for the Brodyland empire, including the bar
at the boutique hotel Brody House.

EAST ASIA & THE PACIFIC

INGREDIENTS

50 ml (1¾ fl oz) Absolut Elyx vodka

10 ml (⅓ fl oz) Peach and Nectarine
   Mancino Secco Vermouth Infusion*

2 dashes of orange bitters

3 olives or a lemon twist, to garnish

*For the Vermouth Infusion
(makes 700 ml/24 fl oz):*

1 peach, stoned (pitted) and cut
   into 6 slices

1 nectarine, stoned (pitted) and
   cut into 6 slices

700 ml (24 fl oz) Mancino Secco

METHOD

For the Vermouth Infusion, combine
the sliced peach and nectarine
with the Mancino Secco, cover and
refrigerate for 24 hours. Strain into
a clean container and the vermouth
infusion is ready to use.

To make the cocktail, add the
ingredients to a mixing glass and
top with ice, then stir for about
20 seconds. Double strain into a
chilled Martini glass and finish with
a garnish of olives or a lemon twist.

It would be foolish to come all the way to
Sydney and not spend ample time basking
within a sight line to the Sydney Opera House.
That's why many travellers plot an evening,
or an afternoon tea, at Blu Bar on 36. From
the 36th floor of the Shangri-La, it feels as
if you are floating over the concrete, shell-
shaped architectural wonder. Together with
the Sydney Harbour Bridge, it's a scene that
simply wows.

The Shangri-La opened in the Rocks area
in 2003. Although guests swoon over the
marble baths and floral patterns splashed
across headboards and carpets, it's the bar
that is likely their favourite aspect of the hotel.
Martinis are an art form here, and there seems
to be at least one on every table, but the
originals also shine. Begin with a 'Two At Most'
(Del Maguey Vida mezcal, yellow Chartreuse,
lime, falernum, absinthe rinse) and end with
the 'GPS', a fusion of Laphroaig, Campari and
Dubonnet. The cocktails are as commendable
as what lies outside the glass walls.

No. 47

36 Above Martini

BLU BAR ON 36
AT SHANGRI-LA,
SYDNEY, AUSTRALIA

LIGHTING
AS
ARTISTIC
NARRATIVE

Partners Greg Bradshaw, Adam Farmerie, William Harris and Kristina O'Neal founded AvroKO in 2001; since then, the design and concept firm has expanded from its New York base to studios in Bangkok, San Francisco and London. A force on the global hospitality scene, AvroKO has designed such Asian hotel bars as Charles H. at Four Seasons Hotel Seoul, Jing at The Temple House in Chengdu, Terrible Baby at Eaton HK in Hong Kong, and UNION and Superfly at The Opposite House in Beijing. Marvellous lighting, woven throughout AvroKO projects, is crucial to the quartet's artistic process. As AvroKO delineates here, this element – all too often neglected in bar settings – is a chance to tell a meaningful story.

Lighting is one of the strongest narrative creators in bar atmospheres. It can create mystery, incite delight or even encourage a particular mood. It can even literally be the story in the room. For us, these are all enticing aspects of the power of lighting design.

We use numerous strategies to create lighting that serves as both art and narrative support. So many designers can make beautiful things, but infusing lighting with a sense of story that creates a deeper connection and sense of meaning is a wonderful challenge and a necessary fuel for an ambitious designer. Abstractly illustrating a story allows guests room for their own interpretation of a piece or the experience the lighting is creating. This kinship can become poetic, with the guests being active participants and, in a sense, creative collaborators in the completion of the statement. When guests can be part of the dialogue, it is that much more satisfying and stimulating.

Lighting also becomes successful as art when there is a sense of awe and delight. Unconventional materials and shapes, unexpected locations, and the wonder of scale can all be employed to great effect; encouraging people to stop and engage, without drowning out the rest of the experience.

Finally, helping people feel physically and emotionally better through proper lighting design is vital. Typically, this includes finding ways to cast a warm glow while also allowing the light to be soft and welcoming. Proper lighting also helps define a space for guests, crafting their journey and creating a sense of place and grounding.

For example, at Nan Bei, a contemporary Chinese restaurant on the 19th floor of the Rosewood hotel in Bangkok with a beautiful, monolithic bar crafted from Portoro Gold marble with satin brass trim detailing, we employed ephemeral lighting design in a dramatic installation to greet guests as they arrive. This installation is an abstraction of a piece of the narrative we were using as inspiration for the interior design as a whole, which was based on the Chinese legend of the Weaver Girl and the Cowherd. As legend has it, the Weaver Girl, who resided in heaven, came down to earth and fell in love with the Cowherd. However, their love was forbidden, and they were only allowed to meet once a year by crossing the night sky over a bridge of magpies.

In the grand open atrium, as a whimsical illustration of this meeting, we crafted over 800 hand-folded 'magpies' out of thin brass metal mesh. These were then hung to create a subtle, arching bridge form. Thousands of warm, glittering LED lights were then installed seven metres high to fill out the space, in essence creating an ethereal night sky. The reflective glass of the surrounding corridors reflects the glowing installation beautifully, creating a magical sense of never-ending expanse. To frame the artwork, we created a modern moon-gate screen, within which we installed a curving upholstered bench. Interactivity is also quite important to us, and with the addition of the bench, curious guests can sit and become part of the piece itself. The resulting effect has become one of the most photographed areas of the restaurant and is now a signature element of the space and the brand.

create mystery,
incite delight

...

a deeper
connection and sense
of meaning

...

wonder of scale

BEHIND THE BAR

6

No. 48

QT G&T

THE ROOFTOP AT QT,
QT MELBOURNE,
AUSTRALIA

INGREDIENTS

2 slices of cucumber
45 ml (1½ fl oz) Tanqueray gin
15 ml (½ fl oz) St-Germain liqueur
15 ml (½ fl oz) freshly squeezed
** lime juice**
15 ml (½ fl oz) simple syrup
** (page 11)**
tonic water, to top up

METHOD

Muddle the cucumber in the
bottom of a highball glass. Add
the gin, St-Germain, lime juice
and syrup, then add ice and top
up with tonic water, stirring it
into the drink with a bar spoon.

Melbourne's bar scene is ruled by rooftops.
Every night, locals head outdoors and on high,
carousing with their crew as the city opens up
wide below them. It doesn't take much for a
rooftop bar to sing; the constant crowds, who
hop from venue to venue, are testament to the
popularity of guzzling atop a building. Every
once in a while, though, you stumble upon a
bar that doesn't just rest on its handsome
views, and instead brings panache to what
often feels ordinary. QT Melbourne's indoor-
outdoor The Rooftop at QT is one of them. As
part of the quirky, art- and design-centric
QT Hotels & Resorts portfolio, QT Melbourne
values aesthetics and the rooftop – one of the
hugest layouts in the city – follows suit. The
bar, wrapped in glistening green brick-style
tiles and harmonised with lots of hanging
plants, is a beauty. Nestle up against pillows
at one of the candle-lit tables and order fish
tacos with a Vanilla Passionfruit Pisco Sour
or the 'Bullet Train to Spain' (Bulleit bourbon,
Pedro Ximénez sherry, orgeat, lemon and
kaffir lime leaves). Even though DJs only
make appearances for special events, there
is the energy of a pulsating party up here on
weekends. Luckily, it never sacrifices cheer.

No. 49

The Remedy

PAPER DAISY
AT HALCYON HOUSE,
CABARITA BEACH,
AUSTRALIA

INGREDIENTS

**4 mixed seasonal berries,
plus extra to garnish**
**60 ml (2 fl oz) dry gin (the bar uses
Brookie's Byron, distilled in Byron
Bay and made with Australian
botanicals)**
**20 ml (⅔ fl oz) freshly squeezed
lemon juice**
20 ml (⅔ fl oz) Mixed Berry Shrub*
plain kombucha, to top up
fresh mint sprig, to garnish

***For the Mixed Berry Shrub
(makes 700 ml/24 fl oz):**
100 g (3½ oz) blueberries
100 g (3½ oz) blackberries
100 g (3½ oz) raspberries
500 g (1 lb 2 oz) white sugar
500 ml (17 fl oz) apple cider vinegar

METHOD

For the Mixed Berry Shrub, muddle
the berries in a 1 litre (34 fl oz) jar.
Add the sugar and vinegar, cover and
let it sit for 1 week. Strain into a clean
bottle or jar. It will keep for 3 months.
 To make the cocktail, softly muddle
the berries in the bottom of a Boston
glass, just enough to burst open the
fruit. Add a little crushed ice, along
with the gin, lemon juice and shrub
and stir. Top with kombucha and
garnish with more crushed ice,
a mint sprig and berries.

Cabarita Beach, some 90 minutes south of
Brisbane, epitomises the concept of holiday.
There is no choice but to chill out here on the
east coast of Australia, and a stay at Halcyon
House almost demands it. An upscale beach
house stocked with vintage furniture and
decorated with upholstered fabric walls and
blue-and-white tiles, it was opened in 2015 by
two visionary sisters who saw great promise
in this old surfer motel. Guests do, too. They
spend mornings taking surf lessons or doing
beachside yoga, then after they've gone hot-
air ballooning over Mount Warning or walking
through a remnant of coastal rainforest to
Norries Headland, they are ready to laze about
in the Halcyon House pool that smacks of Old
Hollywood. There is another stop before calling
it a night, though: Paper Daisy. Crammed
with artwork, Halcyon House's sun-streaked
restaurant is smart yet homey. Locals are
also smitten with the place, even if it's only to
imbibe at the all-white bar. Cocktails including
the 'Spicy Tryst' (chilli-infused Grey Goose
vodka, lime juice, burnt-orange syrup, mango
nectar, passion-fruit pulp) and 'Down the
Garden Path' (Four Pillars Rare dry gin, basil-
and-mint shrub, cucumber, lemon juice, basil-
and-grapefruit soda) precisely summarise the
Halcyon House ethos.

No. 50

Spirit of Virtues

EICHARDT'S BAR
AT EICHARDT'S PRIVATE
HOTEL, QUEENSTOWN,
NEW ZEALAND

Created by Shaun White

INGREDIENTS

30 ml (1 fl oz) Maker's Mark bourbon
30 ml (1 fl oz) Amaro Montenegro
10 ml (⅓ fl oz) Aperol
2 dashes of hopped grapefruit bitters
2 pared strips of lemon zest
twist of lemon zest, to garnish

METHOD

Add the bourbon, amaro, Aperol, bitters and 1 strip of the lemon zest to a mixing glass and stir gently for 10–15 seconds. Strain into a chilled Martini glass or coupe. Express the oils from the other strip of lemon zest over the drink. Finish with a twist of lemon zest.

Queenstown, on the South Island of New Zealand, is where the adventurous come out to play, getting their kicks from bungee jumping, paragliding and abseiling. In the 1860s, that adrenaline rush was achieved in another form: prospecting for gold. During that prosperous era, a woolshed was converted into a hotel; by 1869, when tourism replaced the dispersing miners, Albert Eichardt was sole proprietor. Located on the shores of Lake Wakatipu, Eichardt's Private Hotel remains in the embrace of tourists, except they now embark on yacht cruises, dig into lamb shoulder with pinot-noir jus for two at the Grille, and consider Eichardt's Bar their living room. This is where they lean back in banquettes against mirror-lined stone, grazing on pork-cheek croquettes rolled in wild thyme breadcrumbs. Often, the cocktails will have a culinary bent. Woodford Reserve bourbon might get smoked with Manuka honey, or rye whiskey infused with dates. Topped with homemade blood orange and thyme sorbet, the 'Sangroni' (gin, Campari, thyme syrup) is a merry excuse to sit by the fire just a tad longer.

EICHARDT'S PRIVATE HOTEL
QUEENSTOWN, NEW ZEALAND

EICHARDT'S   PRIVATE   HOTEL.

EAST ASIA & THE PACIFIC

HOTEL CONTACTS

THE AMERICAS

Belmond Copacabana Palace
Avenida Atlântica 1702, Rio de Janeiro
belmond.com

The Carlyle, a Rosewood Hotel
35 E. 76th Street, New York
rosewoodhotels.com

Country Club Lima Hotel
Calle Los Eucaliptos 590, San Isidro, Peru
countryclublimahotel.com

Four Seasons Hotel Mexico City
Av. Paseo de la Reforma 500
fourseasons.com

The Hollywood Roosevelt
7000 Hollywood Boulevard, Los Angeles
thehollywoodroosevelt.com

Hotel Commonwealth
500 Commonwealth Avenue, Boston
hotelcommonwealth.com

Hotel Monteleone
214 Royal Street, New Orleans
hotelmonteleone.com

Hotel Nacional de Cuba
Calle 21 y O, Vedado, Plaza, Havana
hotelnacionaldecuba.com

**InterContinental The Willard
Washington, DC**
1401 Pennsylvania Avenue NW
ihg.com

The NoMad Hotel
1170 Broadway, New York
thenomadhotel.com

Rockhouse Hotel & Spa
W End Road, Negril, Jamaica
rockhouse.com

St Regis New York
2 E. 55th Street
marriott.com

Wedgewood Hotel & Spa
845 Hornby Street, Vancouver
wedgewoodhotel.com

EUROPE

Badrutt's Palace
Via Serlas 27, St Moritz
badruttspalace.com

Belmond Grand Hotel Europe
Mikhaylovskaya Ulitsa 1/7,
St Petersburg
belmond.com

The Connaught
Carlos Place, London
the-connaught.co.uk

**The Gritti Palace, a Luxury
Collection Hotel**
Campo Santa Maria del Giglio, Venice
marriott.com

Hotel am Steinplatz, Autograph Collection, Berlin
Steinplatz 4
hotelsteinplatz.com

Hôtel de Paris Monte-Carlo
Place du Casino, Monaco
montecarlosbm.com

Hotel de Russie
Via del Babuino 9, Rome
roccofortehotels.com

Le Meurice
228 Rue de Rivoli, Paris
dorchestercollection.com

Nimb Hotel
Bernstorffsgade 5, Copenhagen
nimb.dk

Pulitzer Amsterdam
Prinsengracht 323
pulitzeramsterdam.com

Ritz Paris
15 Place Vendôme
ritzparis.com

The Savoy
Strand, London
thesavoylondon.com

The Stafford London
16-18 St James's Place
thestaffordlondon.com

The Thief
Landgangen 1, Oslo
thethief.com

The Westin Palace, Madrid
Plaza de las Cortes 7
marriott.com

THE MIDDLE EAST, AFRICA, SOUTH ASIA, INDIA

Burj Al Arab Jumeirah
Jumeirah Street, Dubai
jumeirah.com

Çırağan Palace Kempinski
Çırağan Caddesi 32, Istanbul
kempinksi.com

La Mamounia
Avenue Bab Jdid, Marrakech
mamounia.com

The Norman Tel Aviv
23-25 Nachmani Street
thenorman.com

The Oberoi, New Delhi
Dr Zakir Hussain Marg, Delhi Golf Club
oberoihotels.com

The Royal Livingstone Victoria Falls Zambia Hotel by Anantara
Mosi-oa-Tunya Road
anantara.com

Sarova Stanley
Kenyatta Avenue and Kimathi
Street junction, Nairobi
sarovahotels.com

The Silo Hotel
Silo Square, Victoria & Alfred
Waterfront, Cape Town
theroyalportfolio.com

W Maldives
Fesdu Island North Ari Atoll,
Marriott.com

ASIA AND THE PACIFIC

Eichardt's Private Hotel
2 Marine Parade, Queenstown,
New Zealand
eichardts.com

Four Seasons Hotel Seoul
97 Saemunan-ro
fourseasons.com

Halcyon House
21 Cypress Crescent,
Cabarita Beach,
Australia
halcyonhouse.com.au

Hilton Kuala Lumpur
3 Jalan Stesen Sentral
hilton.com

Imperial Hotel, Tokyo
1 Chome-1-1 Uchisaiwaichō
imperialhotel.co.jp

Island Shangri-La, Hong Kong
Supreme Court Road
shangri-la.com

Mandarin Oriental, Bangkok
48 Oriental Avenue
mandarinoriental.com

Park Hyatt Tokyo
3-7-1-2 Nishi-Shinjuku
hyatt.com

QT Melbourne
133 Russell Street
qthotels.com

Raffles Singapore
1 Beach Road
raffles.com

Regent Singapore
1 Cuscaden Road
regenthotels.com

Shangri-La Hotel, Sydney
176 Cumberland Street
shangri-la.com

Waldorf Astoria Shanghai On the Bund
2 Zhongshan East 1st Rd
waldorfastoriashanghai.com

About the Author

Alia Akkam's fascination with hotels began as a child when her father returned home from his countless business trips to Asia with a slew of miniature shampoo bottles and Hilton-emblazoned towels.

Born in New York, in the vibrant, multi-cultural borough of Queens – a place for which she still harbours an intense love – Alia is most drawn to urban settings, wandering aimlessly through crowded streets, gorging on local specialties in small, boisterous restaurants and observing quirky characters along the way.

Her childhood and adolescent years spent on Long Island, then, were steeped in wanderlust-fuelled daydreams, spinning the retro globe stashed in the upstairs storage room and plucking the Funk & Wagnalls Hammond World Atlas off a shelf in the living room wall unit to pore over images of international flags.

With a penchant for writing short stories as a kid, Alia headed to the University of South Carolina's journalism school with dreams of becoming an advertising copywriter and moving to Europe. The former goal morphed into a career writing about restaurants, bars, travel and design; the latter eventually happened in 2015. After years of working in New York, Alia adventurously moved to Budapest – a city where she knew no one and didn't speak a lick of Hungarian. Now her days of writing are regularly interspersed with Danube strolls and copious amounts of sponge cake consumption in Old World cafés.

Both an architecture and culture geek, Alia is smitten with Art Deco buildings, London's theatre scene, French New Wave films and street art. A devoted nostalgist, she's happiest imbibing in a historic hotel lobby or eating baked ziti in a red leather booth at an old Italian restaurant, tunes by 1960s girl groups playing in the background.

Acknowledgements

So many people lent their time, their savvy and, in many cases, their recipes to this book, and I am indebted to them. To all the bartenders who generously shared their creations, particularly ms franky marshall and Julia Momose for whipping up delicious drinks specifically for this book, and the publicists who graciously answered my endless questions, I tip my hat to you.

To all the folks who lent their words, including the AvroKO team, Jeff 'Beachbum' Berry, Martin Brudnizki, Frank Caiafa, Ryan Chetiyawardana, Carlos Couturier, Alex Day, Meaghan Dorman, Jeffrey Morgenthaler, Gabe Orta, Christy Pope, David Rockwell, Mike Ryan, Audrey Saunders, Chad Solomon and Elad Zvi, thank you for elevating this book with your industry expertise.

Without the help of bar whiz Dez O'Connell – one of the first friends I made in Budapest, fittingly over a Daiquiri – this book would not have been possible. He sourced ingredients, tested recipes and even lent one of his own to this collection, while offering smart suggestions throughout the journey, and for that I am grateful.

I would also like to toast the amazing Hardie Grant Books team, especially my editor, the sharp, patient Eila Purvis, as well as designer Claire Warner and illustrator Evi-O.Studio, who did a smashing job capturing the transporting magic and whimsy of hotel bars through their designs.

There are others who must be recognised, too: Molly Ahuja, without whom this book never would have seen the light of day; David Farley, Kayt Mathers and Maureen O'Hare, whose constant support added cheer to the more maddening days; Lisa Mendelson, for her inspiring encouragement; Zsófia Fischer and Krisztina Munkácsi, for getting me to the finish line with their wisdom and positivity; the bar staff at KOLLÁZS for planting that first glorious seed; Julie Besonen and David Bailey, for giving me fairy tale chances all those years ago; the late Bori Budaházi, for showing me how life should be lived; and, of course, Aaron Arrowsmith Taylor, for everything.

Index

Published in 2020 by Hardie Grant Books, an imprint of Hardie Grant Publis⋯

Hardie Grant Books (London)
5th & 6th Floors
52–54 Southwark Street
London SE1 1UN

Hardie Grant Books (Melbourne)
Building 1, 658 Church Street
Richmond, Victoria 3121

hardiegrantbooks.com

British Library Cataloguing-in-Publication Data. A catalogue record for this book is available from the British Library.

Behind the Bar
ISBN: 978-1-78488-332-4

10 9 8 7 6 5 4 3 2 1

Publishing Director: Kate Pollard
Senior Editor: Molly Ahuja
Editor: Eila Purvis
Designer: Claire Warner Studio
Illustrations: Evi-O.Studio | Kait Polkinghorne & Susan Le
Copy-editor: Emily Preece-Morrison
Proofreader: Sharona Selby
Indexer: Cathy Heath

Colour reproduction by p2d
Printed and bound in China by Leo Paper Products Ltd.

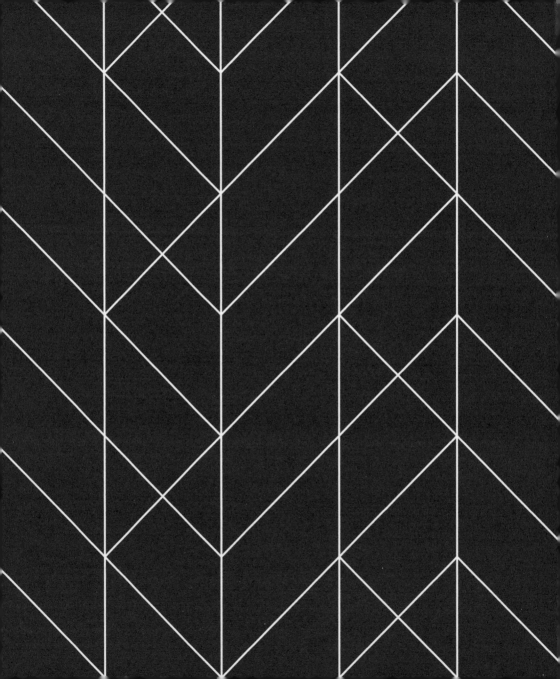